The Poker Night Murders

D. R. TAYLOR

ISBN: 979-8-9862399-0-3 (Paperback)
ISBN: 979-8-9862399-1-0 (eBook)

Editing by Kathleen Strattan
Cover and interior design by John Reinhardt Book Design

Printed in the United States of America

To Do Vo, Lucy and Ali

The First Thursday

JUNE 1, 2017 HAS BEEN a good day for this player, a player in every sense of the word. He spent the morning playing golf. He shot a 76, winning $700 in the process. He just won over $3000 at the weekly poker game where he is a regular. Driving home, he made plans to get laid. He pulls his car into his garage at ten minutes to midnight, time enough to take his dog for a short walk before his female guest arrives. He is winning the game that is his life. But in a few minutes, he will lose everything. Someone will enter the garage and put a bullet in his head.

To know the full story of what happens tonight, it is necessary to rewind six hours and twenty miles. Ronald Turner steps into his poker room at exactly 6:00 p.m. At the center is an octagonal table surrounded by eight swivel chairs with pneumatic lifts. To the right sits a storage cabinet containing a small refrigerator and shelves for poker supplies. A buffet table is positioned next to the storage cabinet. An entertainment center is built into the opposite wall. It houses a surround sound system and a 55-inch television set.

Ronald is a sixty-one-year-old forensic psychiatrist who recently retired. He has played poker regularly for most of his life. His parents taught him to play Five Card Draw, Five Card Stud and Seven Card Stud during family games at the kitchen table. He occasionally played with friends in high school and college. While in medical school and residency he and his classmates took turns hosting low stakes games. Since 1990 he has hosted a weekly game at his home in Hunter's Green, a suburb in an area northeast of Tampa often referred to as New Tampa. By 7:00 eight players will be seated at the table, including the one who will soon be murdered.

For men like Ronald, poker provides a sedentary opportunity to compete. The chance to win money while watching sports and talking trash checks just about every box in the cerebral cortex of the average male. Like a mid-life tree fort, no girls allowed. You can learn a lot about a man from the way he plays poker. It's not just about winning and losing. Is he daring or risk-averse? How does he react when the stakes are high? Does he base decisions on data or instinct? Is he creative or an a-b-c thinker? If you're choosing between two guys to hire, invite them to a poker game.

Ronald was born in Tampa. Before he started school the family moved outside the city limits to Temple Terrace, a small town near the University of South Florida. Ronald and his two younger siblings were raised with the expectation that they would enter professions requiring advanced degrees. Ronald eventually graduated from medical school and became a psychiatrist. His brother Lee took a different path and attended law school. After graduation, Lee worked as a prosecutor in Hillsborough County for eight years before embarking on a career as a criminal defense attorney. Their sister Susan also chose the legal profession. After six years with the Florida Office of the Attorney General, she founded her own firm specializing in wills and estate planning.

As a youth, Ronald wanted to become an athlete rather than a scholar. His father engaged him in athletic contests almost as soon as he could walk. He would usually let Ronald win in order to build his confidence. Later, Ronald was able to dominate his younger siblings. This resulted in his belief that he was athletically invincible. On the rare occasions he experienced defeat he viewed it as a personal failure which must be rectified. His aversion to losing fueled an intense competitive drive that persisted into adulthood.

At 6:28 Ronald is counting and stacking chips. From his left a cat suddenly springs to the top of the table, scattering chips in the process. Ronald claps his hands and yells, "Off!"

The cat hops off the table and scurries to the corner farthest from Ronald, who raises his voice.

"Lisa! Get this frickin' cat out of the poker room!"

Within a minute Ronald's wife appears at the door. She is an attractive, brown-eyed brunette. Some of the patients and staff at the hospital where she works have told her she resembles Sandra Bullock. Not the kind of woman you expect to be married to a guy with a round face, pale skin and rapidly receding gray hair. She bends to gather the cat and smiles, sweetly.

"She's just being curious. You don't have to yell at her."

"Curious, my ass. She made a mess. I don't want to have to deal with her on poker night."

Lisa pets the cat. "Come on, Sneakers. Grumpy old man doesn't want us in his room." They make their exit.

Things have been tense between Ronald and Lisa this week. On Monday, she unexpectedly brought the cat home from a shelter. Ronald is not a cat person, and he does not like surprises. Lisa had been talking about adopting a cat for years, but Ronald thought he had convinced her to wait. Now, he is annoyed by the intrusion. By the time he reconstructs the toppled stacks it is 6:32. He is four minutes behind schedule.

Ronald's childhood fantasy was to exceed the exploits of idols such as Mickey Mantle and Roman Gabriel. In youth sports he was always the starting shortstop on his baseball team and the quarterback of the football team. Based on family history, he expected to grow to a height of six feet or more. However, at age fifteen he reached his full height of five feet ten inches. He was a good high school athlete, but not a great one. During his junior and senior years at King High School he made all-county teams, but never all-state. No major college offered him a football scholarship. His name was not called in the 1974 Major League Baseball draft.

Ronald attended USF on a baseball scholarship. By his sophomore year he realized his career would involve something other than sports. He gave up baseball and decided to become a physician, an ambitious goal that he viewed as a challenge. After getting his undergraduate degree, he attended medical school at the University of Florida. Following graduation he remained at UF to complete a four-year residency program in psychiatry, then a one-year fellowship in forensic psychiatry. The verbal sparring with attorneys while testifying in court provided a satisfying outlet for his competitive nature. After completing his training in 1987 he established a private practice in Tampa.

Soon after opening his practice, Ronald devised a plan to retire after thirty years. The timetable involved dividing his career into ten-year increments. For the first ten years he evaluated and treated patients in his office and at area hospitals. During that time he also built a forensic psychiatry practice, which largely consisted of evaluating criminal defendants for the court system. As his forensic practice expanded, he began to cut back on his clinical practice. He stopped doing hospital work in 1997. He continued to see patients in his office, but he grew more focused on forensic cases. In 2007 he stopped treating patients altogether. For the final ten years he practiced exclusively as a forensic psychiatrist, conducting criminal court evaluations and testifying in court. By 2017 he was ready to retire. He had evaluated almost 10,000 criminal defendants, including more than 200 charged with murder. He had testified in court over 500 times. He stopped accepting new cases, but he remained available to testify regarding defendants he had already evaluated. In April he testified for the last time at the trial of a schizophrenic man accused in the brutal stabbing death of a young woman. At the end of that month, he closed his office. In May he attended the American Psychiatric Association annual meeting in San Diego, mostly to say goodbye to old friends. When he returned to Tampa he looked forward to a retirement highlighted by international travel, reading the great books and hosting Thursday night poker games.

When Ronald lived alone in a Tampa apartment in the late 1980s, he and a group of friends took turns hosting weekly poker games. Most of the other players were psychiatrists and psychologists he met through his practice. Ronald cultivated the activity into an outlet for his competitive drive. If he was going to play, he was determined to win. He read books on poker strategy and learned how to calculate odds. He became a consistent winner. When he built a house in 1990, he chose a model with a bonus room that could be optimized for poker. He began hosting games every Thursday night. Interest in the game eventually exceeded the number of seats available. In addition to eight regular players there were alternates ready to fill a seat in someone's absence. When a regular player moved or dropped out of the game there was always a replacement. Most of the newer players were attorneys Ronald had met through his siblings or his professional activities. The format of the game evolved, and the stakes steadily rose. By 2017 it cost $1000 to buy into the game plus $10 for food, beverages and supplies.

Ronald is a creature of routine. By 6:53 he has completed his usual preparation tasks. Four folding trays have been placed around the table so that one is within easy reach of each seat. Five discs have been loaded into the CD player. Tonight's selection includes Led Zeppelin, Lynrd Skynyrd and the Moody Blues, to be played in alphabetical order. In front of each chair is $1000 worth of poker chips in uniform stacks of red ($5), blue ($10), green ($25) and black ($100). Potato chips, nuts and other snacks are in serving bowls. The refrigerator is stocked with beer and soft drinks. An ice bucket and a pitcher of water are filled and placed on top of the buffet table. The TV set is tuned to the channel broadcasting the Stanley Cup finals. Tonight is Game 2 between the

Nashville Predators and the Pittsburgh Penguins. Ronald counts and shuffles two decks of cards while waiting for his guests to arrive.

For over twenty years the first one through the doorway was usually Jason Bowen. Born and raised in Miami, Jason had a distinguished career as an experimental psychologist. After completing graduate school, he served in the United States Army for twenty years, He advanced to the rank of colonel. During the Vietnam War he was instrumental in developing interrogation techniques designed to extract information from captured enemy soldiers. Following his discharge, he embarked on a second career as a professor and later chairman of the Department of Psychology at the University of Tampa. He met and married a professor eighteen years his junior. After retiring in 2001 he got involved in a variety of community activities, most significantly as a major fundraiser for the Republican Party. For years he was the most successful player in the weekly poker game despite the fact that he was significantly older than the others. He often told them he would stop playing before his skills eroded rather than afford them the opportunity to regain the money he had taken from them. By 2014 the game had become tougher. He decided that reaching eighty years of age was a good stopping point.

At 6:54 Ronald hears a booming voice.

"Helloo, Ron!"

Ronald looks up to see Dick Richardson enter the room. Short and stocky with a gray mustache and beard, the seventy-year-old attorney has been the game's patriarch since Jason stopped playing. Dick was born in a small mining town in northern Kentucky. He attended Princeton University and Yale Law School, where he graduated first in his class. At Yale he was nicknamed "Bluegrass" because of his Appalachian roots. He worked at a law firm in New York for four years before accepting a position at a venerable firm in Tampa. He earned a partnership in record time and eventually became the head of the litigation department. He once hosted his own poker game but accepted an invitation to join Ronald's game as a regular in 2002.

"Hi, Dick. How did you do last weekend?" Dick plays in a $500 buy-in tournament at a local poker room almost every Sunday.

"Finished fourth, cashed for $1100."

"Good job. I hope you saved some for tonight."

Dick smiles as he pours a Diet Pepsi.

Scott Krueger is the next to arrive. He is a fifty-nine-year-old forensic psychologist originally from Boston. After obtaining a Ph.D. in clinical psychology and completing forensic training, he became a professor in the psychology department at USF. Scott is a walking textbook in the field of forensic psychology. In fact, he has published three books as well as scores of scholarly articles on law and mental health. He met Ronald through professional circles in 1987. Scott has been a regular player in the Thursday night game since its inception.

Matt Pardo enters the room right after Scott. Matt is a fifty-six-year-old native of Tampa. While at Tampa Catholic High School he was the most valuable player of a baseball team that won a state championship. He is now the senior partner of one of the largest accounting firms in the city. Matt is a former neighbor who has been a regular in the game since 1992. Like Ronald, he and Scott are of average height and build. Scott has a full beard.

"Hi, guys," says Ronald as Matt and Scott take their seats. "Special promo tonight. High hand gets a free cat."

Scott defers. "I've already got one too many."

Robert Cole and David Epstein arrive at 6:57. Robert is also a Tampa native. At sixty-four he is the game's second oldest player. At six feet four inches and over 250 pounds he cuts an imposing figure at the table. He once worked as an attorney at the law firm where Dick was a senior partner. For the last several years he has headed his own firm, specializing in contract law. Robert has played in the game since 2004.

David is as tall as Robert, but his slender physique reflects his younger days as a college athlete. He is a fifty-eight-year-old child psychologist from Brooklyn. He was able to parlay his basketball talent into a scholarship to St. John's University, where he was a deadly accurate outside shooter. During his senior year he finished third in the Big East in scoring. He might have been first had his career not predated the three-point line. While at St. John's he met his future wife, a middle-distance track star named Janet. She was expected to win two medals at the 1980 Summer Olympics in Moscow until the United States decided to boycott the games. David and Janet married during graduate school. They have lived in Tampa since 1989. David joined Scott, Jason and Ronald as charter members of the Thursday night game beginning in 1990.

"Ron, how was San Diego?" asks David.

"Fine. Not much to tell."

"Did you do anything fun?"

"Went to the zoo. I guess that was the highlight."

"Great zoo," adds Scott. "I've been there twice."

Cody King and Brian Ridge are the last to arrive. Cody is recounting their dinner at Ciccio Cali.

"How many times did that waitress forget to bring your broccoli? I didn't know somebody that young could have Alzheimer's."

Brian grins. "You're so naïve. She just wanted an excuse to keep coming back."

Matt is skeptical. "So, you're saying she just wanted some Brian action?"

Robert chimes in. "Did you at least wait until she cleared the table?"

"Hey, that chick was into me," Brian insists. "She was audibly lubricating." He and Cody slide into their chairs to the sound of laughter.

Cody replaced Jason as a regular in 2014. At forty-two he is the game's youngest player as well as the newest. He was born in Tampa and raised in the upscale Palma Ceia neighborhood. His wealthy parents were killed in a car crash when he was sixteen. His brother, six years his senior, accepted the responsibility of steering Cody into adulthood. A trust fund provided each of them a monthly income of over $20,000. Cody's brother became a minister. He prevailed on Cody to attend college and choose a helping profession. Cody attended USF. He majored in education with a minor in history. His disposable income and penchant for late hours conspired to lead him down a path of substance use. He began using cocaine during the day to maintain alertness in class. At night he drank beer or took sedatives to help him sleep. The addictions persisted after he graduated. He took a position teaching history at Plant High School, his alma mater. As a coach he guided two girls' volleyball teams to state championships. He also enjoyed betting on sports. The cocaine use and the gambling left him with little in the way of savings. Since the NBA playoffs began in April he has been on a historically bad run. By early May he owed a bookie almost $40,000, which he could not pay. He borrowed $50,000 from Brian in order to stay in the action. When Cody sank further into debt, Brian loaned him another $50,000. Cody agreed to repay $10,000 per month coinciding with when he received his trust fund payments on the 15th of each month. The first payment is due in two weeks.

Cody lives in the house he inherited from his parents. He is married to Cindy, a teacher at the same high school. They focus much of their attention on a German shepherd named Radley. Before Cody left the house tonight, he learned that Cindy is pregnant with their first child. As usual, he caught a ride to the game with Brian. Cody's license was suspended in 2015 following his second DUI arrest. Since Brian made a habit of leaving the game early, Cody usually had to summon an Uber for a ride home.

Brian Ridge is a forty-eight-year-old entrepreneur from Kansas. He is the game's wealthiest player. He worked as an executive at IBM and Dell before moving to Tampa and starting his own company. The business specialized in measuring internet traffic for advertisers. When the company went public, Brian's stock options became worth millions. He stepped away from the CEO position in 2009 but he remained on the board of directors and continued to draw a seven-figure salary as a consultant. Brian is the only bachelor among the regular players. His longest continuous relationship has been with Millie, his miniature pinscher. Brian joined the Thursday night game as a regular in 2012 and supplanted Jason as the best player. He also managed to become the least popular member of the group.

The game had always thrived on camaraderie and competitive balance. The regular players liked and respected each other. Most were roughly equal in ability. In the 1990s Ronald began keeping detailed results for each player. Jason was the biggest winner every year. Ronald,

Scott, David and Matt were usually above the break-even point. Most of the money was lost by a series of poor players, each of whom quit the game after a few years. Jason eventually convinced Ronald to stop keeping records. He was concerned that the other players would resent his success if they continued to see it in black and white. He also didn't want a written record of his unreported income. The game became even more competitive after Dick and Robert replaced losing players. That left Frank Walters, a child psychiatrist who worked with David, as the game's only consistent loser.

Frank eventually tired of licking his wounds. He dropped out of the game in 2009. Over the next three years, four alternates subsidized the game. None lasted more than a year. In 2012 Ronald searched for a replacement who could afford to inject cash into the game on an ongoing basis. Robert had done some legal work for Brian and knew he had a lot of disposable income. Brian told Robert he enjoyed poker, but he was not very good at it. Ronald thought Brian sounded like the ideal recruit and invited him to play on a trial basis. Brian lost $3000 the first night. He played almost every hand, often betting recklessly. When bluffing he loudly announced the size of the bet and emphatically put his chips into the pot, a tell the other players quickly noticed. His mood remained upbeat. Losing money did not stop him from telling an endless series of tasteless jokes, which amused the other players. He left early but asked to be allowed to return to recoup his losses. Ronald polled the other players. They voted unanimously to invite Brian to be a regular.

Brian's play was remarkably improved the next week. He folded more often. Almost every time he showed his cards, he had the best hand. His tell disappeared. He didn't try to bluff, or at least he was never caught in the act. Conversely, there were three times he picked off players who tried to bluff him out of a hand. When Jason bet $300 with a busted flush draw, Brian called him with just a pair of Deuces to take down a nice pot. He continued to make jokes, but they weren't as funny now that he was winning.

Brian won over $2000 that night. He continued winning week after week, usually $1000 or more. It soon became apparent that his skill level was well beyond that of the other players, including Jason. Brian eventually revealed that he had cashed in six World Series of Poker events, including a bracelet in Omaha Hi-Lo 8 or Better. The competitive balance of the game shifted dramatically. Jason struggled to break even. The other players almost always lost. Several of them told Ronald that Brian should be disinvited. Jason was the most adamant. Ronald considered it. For the first time in his life, he was a losing player and Brian was clearly the cause. Ronald was angry at the thought of being duped. But he could not bring himself to eject someone from the game for being too good a player.

Jason dropped out of the game in 2014. Brian, aware of the growing animus, offered to help find a replacement who would be a net loser. He played golf at the Palma Ceia Golf and Country Club several times a week. After a round, he and other members often stayed in the clubhouse to play poker. Brian told Ronald some of the guys were lousy players who could afford to lose large sums. He invited Ronald to join them and see for himself. After two sessions, Ronald invited Cody King to become a regular player on a trial basis. He also put Russ Nichols and Bill Mumphrey at the top of the alternate list.

Unlike Brian, Cody was not a hustler. He proved to be a terrible player who restored a sense of balance to the game. He usually lost $1000 or more. Brian remained the only consistent winner, while the others sparred over the middle ground. The ill will toward Brian subsided but remained below the surface. As for Cody, he began to grow weary of Brian needling him for his poor play. Brian even nicknamed Cody "ATM" for the way he dispensed cash. One of the reasons Brian loaned Cody the money to pay his gambling debt was so Cody would not have to drop out of the poker game. Nobody else knows about the loan. Such is the state of the game on the first Thursday in June.

The game is full tonight, so none of the alternates will get a chance to play. Russ Nichols is an attorney who specializes in personal injury cases. His picture and his firm's motto ("I'm with You") can be seen on billboards and buses all over the city. Bill Mumphrey is an attorney whose firm specializes in insurance defense. Both Russ and Bill are in their forties and unmarried. As the alternates with the most seniority, they have been the most frequent stand-ins for absent regulars. They almost always leave with less money than they bring. Bruce Silver is the head of a civil engineering firm. He has been an alternate since 2015. He is a better player than Russ or Bill and has grown impatient in his desire to become a regular. Rick Williams is the newest alternate. He is an attorney whose firm has represented two of the three major sports franchises in the Tampa area. He won the only time he played. He asked if he had to kill somebody to move up on the list, and if anyone had a preference.

Like most home games in the 1990s, the Thursday night game started as a dealer's choice game. Players usually opted to deal Hi-Lo split versions of Seven Card Stud or Omaha. Over the years the maximum bet gradually increased from $1 to $10. After the televised poker boom began in 2003, the format shifted to No Limit Hold 'Em. Instead of a maximum bet, No Limit Hold 'Em has a minimum bet established by what are called blinds. Blinds are so named because the two players to the dealer's left have to post bets before the cards are dealt. The small blind usually posts half the minimum bet, followed by the big blind posting the minimum bet. After the cards are dealt, subsequent players have to bet at least the minimum unless they opt to fold.

No Limit Hold 'Em became popular through televised tournaments such as the World Series of Poker and the World Poker Tour. The difference is that the Thursday night game is a cash game, not a tournament. Cash games differ from tournaments in several ways. In cash games the chips have actual value and can be redeemed for money, as opposed to tournaments where the chips are simply a means of keeping score. In cash games the amount of the blinds does not change, whereas in tournaments the blinds increase as the tournament progresses. In cash games you can lose all your chips and elect to buy more, as opposed to most tournaments in which losing all your chips means you are finished. Finally, cash games end when the players decide to stop, unlike tournaments which end when one player has all the chips. The Thursday night game ends promptly at midnight, although players are free to leave earlier.

It has been said that No Limit Hold 'Em takes a minute to learn and a lifetime to master, notwithstanding the fact that most of the best players are under thirty. The Thursday night game is a 5-10 game. At the start of each hand, the player to the dealer's left posts a $5 small blind. The player to his left posts a $10 big blind. All players are dealt two cards face down, known as hole cards. The hole cards comprise the starting hand. Players not in the blinds look at their cards before deciding whether to put money in the pot. Starting with the player to the left of the big blind, the action moves clockwise around the table as each player can fold, limp (call) for $10 or raise to $20 or more. A usual raise is to $30 or $40, but a player is free to raise more. Once the action is complete, three community cards are dealt. This is known as the flop. There is another round of betting starting with the first player to the dealer's left who is still in the hand. Similar rounds of betting occur after the fourth and fifth community cards. The fourth card is known as the turn. The fifth card is called the river. Any time a player bets or raises and nobody calls, that player wins all the money in the pot. If all cards have been dealt and the betting is done, the player with the best hand wins the pot. Players use any combination of their two hole cards and the five on the board to make their best hand.

Although No Limit is part of the game's title, the amount a player can bet or raise is actually limited to the amount of chips he has. Players may buy additional chips between hands, but once the cards have been dealt they can play only the chips in front of them. When a player bets all of his chips it is called being "all in."

Certain starting hands are known as named hands. An Ace with a King (AK) is called Big Slick. Pocket Nines (99) is known as Wayne Gretsky. A Jack and a 4 (J4) is referred to as Flat Tire, i.e., What's a jack for? After the first hand, Brian announces that he folded Updog. Cody snickers as Dick takes the bait.

"What's Updog?"

"Not much, Dog," Brian replies. "What's up with you?" A few of the players laugh. Most groan.

In the long run poker is a game of skill. Given enough time, the best players will come out ahead and the worst players will be net losers. However, even good players can lose if they have an unlucky night. Conversely, a poor player can win if he gets lucky. After Phil Hellmuth was eliminated from a televised tournament in 2006, he famously consoled himself on camera by saying "I guess if luck weren't involved, I'd win every time."

Dick deals the third hand. Robert and David post the blinds. Cody is in first position, also known as "under the gun." He limps with a Queen and an 8 of different suits, or Q8 off-suit. This is a marginal starting hand that should usually be folded. Brian and Matt fold. Scott calls $10 with the Queen and Jack of diamonds, referred to as QJ suited. When both hole cards are the same suit, the hand is referred to as suited. Ronald and Dick fold. It is $5 for Robert to call from the small blind, but he folds 93 off-suit. In the big blind David looks down at K6 off-suit, a hand not nearly good enough to raise. He checks, not wanting to invest more than the $10 he was obligated to post. The pot is $35. The flop is:

Both Cody and Scott have a pair of Queens, but Scott's Jack kicker puts him ahead of Cody's 8. David has nothing and checks. Cody thinks he has the best hand and bets $25. Scott calls. David folds. The pot is $85.

Ronald has seen this movie many times. It usually ends with Cody losing out on a pot he built. Nobody raised before the flop, so it's unlikely that either player has AA, KK or QQ. There is no flush or straight draw. Both players probably have a Queen for top pair. Ronald knows Scott would have folded before the flop if his kicker were not Ten or better. Cody, on the other hand, might see the flop with a Queen and almost any kicker. He would have raised with AQ or KQ, so those hands can be ruled out. That means his kicker could be as high as a Jack or as low as a Deuce. Ronald's money is on Scott.

The turn card is the 5 of hearts. The board is:

Scott still has the best hand, but Cody bets $50. Scott calls. The pot is $185. Only three cards in the deck can help Cody. He needs an 8.

The river card is the 8 of spades. The board is:

Cody now has two pair. He bets $120. Scott thinks for a moment before calling. It's time to turn over the cards. Cody proudly shows his two pair. Scott groans, reveals his hand and tosses the cards into the muck (discards). Some of the players voice sympathy for Scott getting unlucky. Only Brian directs his comments to Cody.

"A three-outer on the river to win a hand he should have folded before the flop! ATM is like Phil Hellmuth's idiot brother. If it weren't for luck he'd lose every time." A few of the players grimace. Cody's broad smile disappears. Nothing more is said for a few minutes.

At 7:46 the sounds of "Stairway to Heaven" fill the room. Scott attempts to mimic the percussion motions of John Bonham. Brian feels the need to say something funny.

"Last week I was on a date with a twenty-four-year-old. She heard this song on the radio and asked if that was Fred Zeppelin."

Robert laughs, then proposes a moment of silence for the recently departed Gregg Allman. "Ron?" he asks. "Are you going to insert the Allman Brothers CD into the rotation tonight?"

Robert smiles as Ronald frowns. Robert knew the answer before he asked the question.

"We'll get around to it in a few weeks. He'll still be dead."

Most hands play out without much drama. There are a few bets and somebody takes a modest pot without showing their cards. Every now and then a big hand occurs which can make or break a player's night. David and Matt are about to tangle in such a hand.

It is David's turn to deal. A button marked "Dealer" is placed in front of him, which is why dealing is also known as being "on the button." Cody and Brian are the blinds. Matt, acting first, raises to $35. Scott, Ronald, Dick and Robert fold. David looks at his cards and re-raises to $100. Cody and Brian fold from the blinds. Matt pauses before calling the additional $65. The pot is $215. Both players have about $900 remaining. The flop is:

Matt checks. David bets $150. Matt counts his stack before announcing "All in." David immediately calls and shows KK. Matt sighs and shows TT. Both players have a pocket pair, meaning their hole cards formed a pair. Both matched their pocket pair on the flop to make three of a kind, also known as a set.

When holding a pocket pair, the probability of flopping a set is about 12%. When two players have a pocket pair, the odds of both flopping a set are about 1%. This scenario is known as set over set. It is a nightmare for the player with the lower set. There is no reason to think you're beat and no way to fold. At this point Matt is ahead of every starting hand except KK. Now, only the last Ten in the deck can save him. The probability of that Ten appearing on the turn or the river is less than 5%.

The turn is a 5 and the river is a 9. David's three Kings hold up. He collects the pot of over $2000. Matt calmly reaches for $1000 to buy more chips.

By 8:27 the conversation has turned to politics. Among the group only David and Cody count themselves as Trump supporters. David had long admired him from his career as a Manhattan developer. Cody's support is based strictly on self-interest. He reasoned that he would be allowed to keep more of his income by a Trump administration than by any Democrat. Ronald referred to the president as Steatorrhea, a medical term for fecal matter with a high fat content. He and the other players voted for Crooked Hillary with the exception of Dick, who voted for a third-party candidate. According to Dick, "If you voted for Hillary, you have no balls. If you voted for Trump, you have no brain."

Cody kicks it off. "Yesterday I heard Rush Limbaugh explain why most men didn't vote for Crooked Hillary. She reminded them of their ex-wife."

"Did anyone read her quotes about the election?" asks David. "She blames Comey and the Russians."

Cody responds, "Of course she does. She'll say anything other than admit people don't like her because she's a lying bitch."

Scott recoils. "Hey! No reason for misogyny."

Others start to challenge the insult. Ronald squirms in his seat. He sees that the situation is about to escalate and slow the pace of the game. Dick tries to change the subject.

"Did you hear Joe Biden is launching a PAC? He says he's not running, but why else would he do it?"

"If he lives that long," replies Matt. "Even then he'd be four years too late to save us from this freak show."

Cody returns to Scott's comment. "How am I a misogynist? Have you guys ever invited a woman to this game?" He lifts his bottle of Amber Bock and takes a swallow.

Ronald chuckles as David answers. "We talked about it a while back, but we didn't know any women who would agree to the conditions."

"What conditions?" asks Brian.

"Their chips would only be worth 80 cents on the dollar."

Cody almost spits out his beer.

Three kinds of starting hands are usually worth playing. The first is a pocket pair. AA is the best starting hand, followed by KK, QQ, etc. The second category includes unpaired big cards such as AJ or KQ, especially if they are suited. The third group consists of medium-sized, adjacent cards of the same suit, also known as suited connectors. Examples are 98 of diamonds and 65 of clubs. The value of suited connectors lies in their potential to make flushes or straights. On a board of 5 6 7 a player holding 98 has the best possible hand, a straight to the 9. The best possible hand is known as "the nuts." When it's time to turn over the cards, having the nuts is an enviable place to be.

At 8:44 David is up over $1500. Brian and Cody are up about $200 each. Matt and Scott are down. The other players are about even. Ronald deals the cards. Dick and Robert post the blinds. David folds. Cody looks at his cards and sees the Ace and Queen of spades (AQ suited), a strong starting hand. He raises to $30. Brian calls. Matt, Scott and Ronald fold. Dick and Robert fold from the blinds. The pot is $75. The flop is:

Cody is pretty happy with this flop. He has an Ace high flush draw and two overcards, meaning both are bigger than any card on the board. Even if he doesn't get a spade for the flush, he can pair his Ace or his Queen for top pair. Either would probably give him the best hand. He bets $50. He would be okay with Brian folding. Brian thinks before calling. The pot is $175.

The turn card is the 9 of spades. The board is:

Cody can barely contain his glee. He has an Ace high flush! Now his focus shifts to getting as many chips from Brian as he can. He needs to get more money into the pot, but he doesn't want Brian to fold. Cody settles on a bet size of $100. Brian quickly calls. The pot is $375.

Cody tries to deduce Brian's hand. His primary concern is that Brian has a set with 55, 88, JJ or 99. If that's the case, Brian would probably call but not raise on a board containing three cards of the same suit because he's losing to a flush. If the board pairs on the river his set would improve to a full house or four of a kind, both of which would beat a flush. Another possibility is a smaller flush. That would be ideal for Cody. His only concern is whether the board pairs.

The river card is the 3 of diamonds. The board is:

Cody breathes a sigh of relief. The board did not pair, meaning Brian cannot have a full house. Cody tries to decide the optimal bet size to extract the maximum amount of money from his victim. He wants to bet the largest amount that Brian will call. Both players have a little over $1000 left, too much to go all in. Cody settles on $180. The bet is less than half the size of the pot, but Cody is afraid Brian would fold to a larger bet. He announces the bet and puts the chips into the pot.

Brian casts a steely gaze on his opponent. Cody has seen that look. Brian is going to try to push him out of the hand. After what seems like an eternity, Brian says "Raise." He puts $450 into the pot.

"All in!" Cody blurts out. Brian deliberately puts the rest of his chips into the pot without saying a word. Cody triumphantly shows his cards and exclaims, "I have the nuts!"

Brian looks at Cody, smiles and asks, "Are you sure?" He slowly turns over the 7 of spades and the 6 of spades. Cody looks at the cards and back at the board. "Oh f---!" he shrieks. Brian has a straight flush! Cody hadn't seen that a straight flush was possible. In this case, the Ace high flush was the second nuts.

The other players gasp and stare at the cards in astonishment. Cody looks shellshocked. Brian rakes in the $2415 pot. While stacking the chips he cackles. "He didn't have to take that last raise. A lot of players would have seen they were beat by a straight flush, but not ATM."

Cody stays silent, but Scott responds angrily. "It's bad enough you slow-roll him after a beat like that! Do you have to twist the knife?" Others murmur in agreement. Brian smiles and continues stacking chips.

Still stunned, Cody reaches into his pocket for $1000 to buy more chips. He will lose those by the end of the evening. He gulps what's left of his second beer and trudges to the refrigerator to get another.

It is 9:06. The hockey game is tied 1–1 at the end of the first period. During the intermission, the camera zooms in on a well-endowed female fan.

Robert remarks, "At least she'll never die from drowning."

David adds, "I don't know how she can stand up without tipping over."

"I know how she feels," replies Brian. "I carry a lot of crotch weight." The comment elicits eyerolls.

It is Cody's turn to deal. Brian and Matt are the blinds. Scott folds under the gun. Ronald limps with T9 of hearts. Dick and Robert call. David folds. Cody calls, as usual. Brian folds and Matt checks. Five players will see the flop, much to Ronald's delight. Suited connectors play well in multi-way hands, and he did not have to call a raise. The pot is $55. The flop is:

Matt checks. The flop missed Ronald and he checks as well. Dick immediately bets $35. Robert calls. Cody, Matt and Ronald fold. The pot is $125.

The turn is the 3 of clubs. The board is:

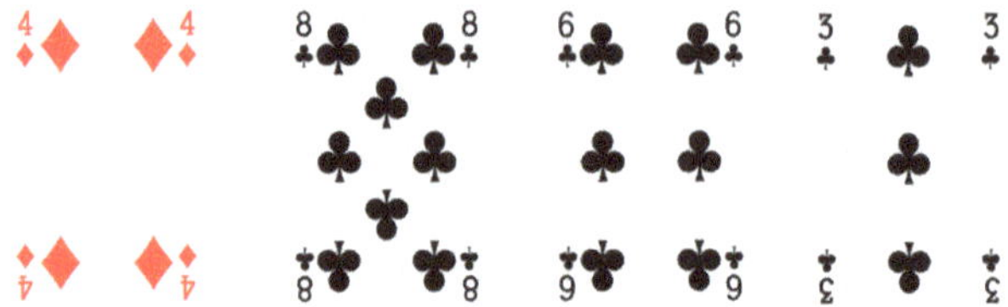

Dick checks. Robert thinks for a moment, then checks as well. The river card is the 4 of hearts. The board is:

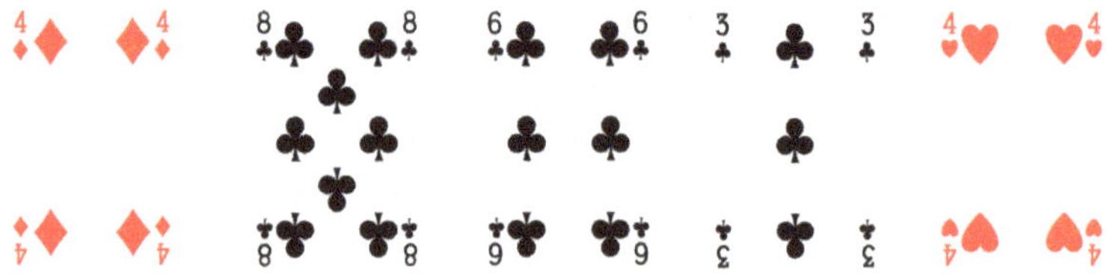

Now Dick bets $75. Robert announces, "Raise." He makes it $200. Back to Dick, who responds, "Raise to 500."

Robert is befuddled. "What did you hit, Bluegrass?" He contemplates for over two minutes.

Finally, Brian breaks the silence. "Whaddya think, Bob? Is he full or full of shit?"

"One player to a hand!" snaps Ronald.

Chastened, Brian nods but does not apologize. He has committed a breach of poker etiquette by pointing out the possibility of a full house due to the board being paired. Although both Dick and Robert are aware of this, those not in the hand should refrain from speculating aloud about who has what hand. It is a common faux pas among inexperienced players, but Brian knows better.

Finally, Robert calls and shows 66. But Dick shows 44. Both players flopped a set. The betting wasn't crazy on the flop because both could be beat by a straight or a bigger set. Both players checked the turn because the possibility of a club flush was added. On the river, Robert made a full house but Dick made quad Fours. Robert saved money by not raising again.

"I didn't see that coming," says Robert. "I was beat by Four-Four and Eight-Eight. End of list."

"I'll tell you my secret," replies Dick. "Always make your hand on the river. That way, nobody can draw out on you." Even Robert laughs.

A few minutes later, Brian relates an anecdote about a neighbor whose cat lost a tail in a lawn mowing accident. He mentions that the neighbor took the cat to Wal-Mart.

"Why did she do that?" Matt asks, incredulously.

"Because they're the world's largest re-tailer." Nobody laughs.

At 9:45 Matt is on the button. Scott and Ronald post the blinds. Dick and Robert fold. David looks down at AJ. He raises to $35. Cody uncharacteristically folds. Brian looks at his cards and re-raises to $100. Matt, Scott and Ronald quickly fold in succession.

David stares at Brian. He knows Brian could be making this play with garbage. On the other hand, David is in bad shape if Brian has AK or AQ. And Brian will have position on him.

"Do you have a real hand or are you playing position?"

Brian smiles but stays silent. They both know David is going to fold. Finally, David mucks his cards.

One nuance of No Limit Hold 'Em is that it is a game of position. The player acting first is referred to as "out of position." The one acting last is "in position." After the flop, the turn and the river the player in position will always have the opportunity to gain information from the player who acts first. This is a tremendous advantage because it allows him a better chance to assess the strength of his opponent's hand. Before the flop, good players might play marginal hands from late position that they would usually fold from early position.

After a slow start, Ronald is starting to collect chips. He hasn't won any big pots, but he's up over $300 by being patient and winning small to medium-sized pots. It is Dick's turn to deal. Robert and

David post the blinds. Acting first, Cody raises to $30. Brian, Matt and Scott fold.

Ronald is one off the button, also known as the cutoff seat. He looks down at AT. This is a decent starting hand, but it does not usually play well against a raise from early position. When good players raise in that spot, they usually have a high pocket pair or a big Ace such as AK or AQ. AT is an underdog to all of these hands. If Matt or Scott had made a similar raise, Ronald would have folded. But Cody is a loose player who often raises with marginal hands from early position. Ronald also knows that he will have position on Cody for the rest of the hand. He calls $30.

Dick, Robert and David fold. Ronald likes this situation. He is heads up against a poor player, and he is in position with a decent hand. The pot is $75. The flop is:

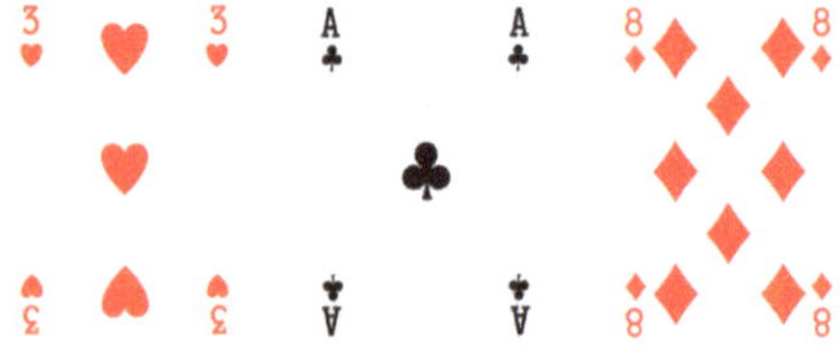

Ronald is pleased with this flop. He has a pair of Aces with a good kicker. He waits for Cody to act, hoping he will tip his hand.

Cody bets $75. The pot-sized bet means Cody wants Ronald to fold. Ronald considers Cody's possible hands. The best-case scenario is that he's making a continuation bet with a pocket pair like JJ or two picture cards such as KQ. Pre-flop raisers often make such bets after a sub-optimal flop, hoping their opponent will fold. AA is the worst-case scenario, but it's unlikely that Cody has the last two Aces in the deck. Ronald would also be in bad shape against 33 or 88. But if Cody had flopped a set, he would probably make a smaller bet to entice Ronald to call. It is even less likely that Cody holds 83. Not even Cody would raise under the gun with 83. His most likely holding is a hand with an Ace. If he has AK, AQ or AJ he has Ronald outkicked. If he has A8 or A3 he has flopped two pair. If Cody has an Ace with any other kicker, Ronald has the best hand. Ronald decides to call and see what happens on the turn. The pot is $225.

The turn is the 8 of spades. The board is:

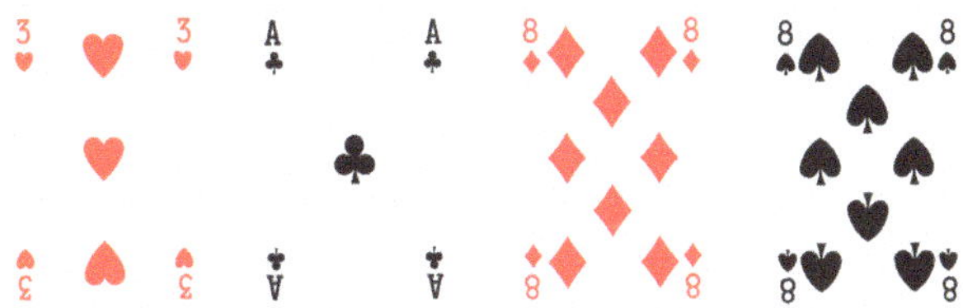

This is a good card for Ronald. It makes it less likely that Cody flopped a set with 88 or two pair with A8. If he flopped two pair with A3 his hand has been "counterfeited." That means his 3 is essentially worthless because he would now have Aces and Eights with a 3 kicker. If that's the case, Ronald is in the lead holding Aces and Eights with a Ten kicker.

Cody bets $120. Ronald believes Cody probably has an Ace. If his kicker is a King, Queen, Jack or Eight he is ahead of Ronald. Otherwise, Ronald is leading. Ronald calls. The pot is $465.

The river card is the 4 of clubs. The board is:

Ronald could hardly ask for a better card. There is virtually no chance that the card helped Cody. Also, the small card means Ronald's Ten kicker plays. Had the card been a King, Queen or Jack the pot would be split if Cody had an Ace and a small card.

Cody checks. Ronald is now certain that Cody has a pocket pair that did not match the board or an Ace with a weak kicker. Either way, Ronald has the best hand. His task now is to decide how large a bet Cody will call. Ronald settles on $250.

Cody pauses for a moment, then unenthusiastically says, "Call." Both players show their hands. Sure enough, Cody has A7 to give him Aces and Eights with a 7 kicker. Ronald's Ten kicker is the difference. He collects the $965 pot, of which $490 is profit. It is his biggest win of the night.

During the fourth hour of play the background hockey game moves to the foreground. After a scoreless second period it's still 1–1. Ten seconds into the third period the Penguins score to take the lead. Cody emits an anguished groan.

Brian can't resist needling his foil. "Guess who bet on the Predators."

A few minutes later the Penguins score twice more in rapid succession. Cody's groans get progressively more subdued. The Penguins hold on to win 4–1 and take a series lead of two games to none. As the horn sounds, Cody is visibly downcast. Brian piles on.

"I have a financial tip for you guys. Ask ATM which way he bet and do the opposite."

Cody has the look of a dog who has been repeatedly whipped by his master. He glares at Brian but says nothing.

At 10:58 Ronald is up over $1000. If he can hold onto his chips for another hour, it will be his first winning session in four weeks. Brian deals the cards. Matt and Scott are the blinds. Ronald looks down at AA. He raises to $40, hoping to thin the herd. Dick, Robert and David fold. Cody calls. Ronald is okay with that. He knows Cody will cough up lots of chips with a losing hand. Then Brian calls. Ronald is not happy about this development. Matt and Scott fold. The pot is $135.

Ronald's hand is at least a 4:1 favorite against all other starting hands. Still, things can get tricky against two opponents. Especially when one of them is Brian. Ronald hopes to end the hand quickly. The flop is:

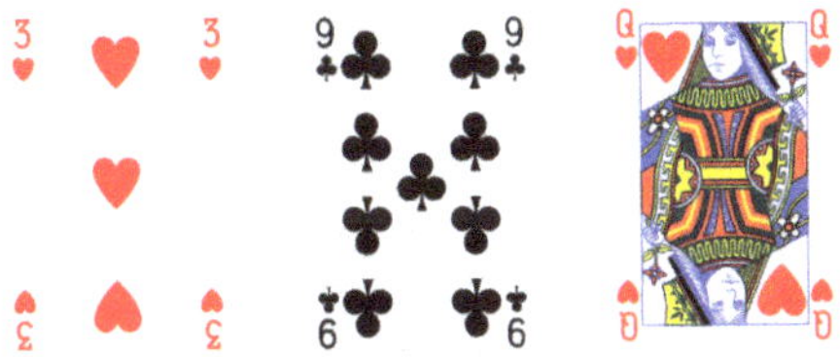

Ronald bets $100. Cody quickly folds. Brian thinks for a moment before calling. Ronald's heart sinks. He does not relish playing heads up out of position against the game's best player.

If Brian holds 33, 99 or QQ he has flopped a set and Ronald is in bad shape. Ronald can eliminate QQ because Brian did not re-raise before the flop. With a set of Nines or Threes, Brian would probably raise rather than call because of the two hearts on the board. If Ronald were holding two hearts, Brian would not want to give him a chance to make a flush without paying for it. Ronald decides Brian has a Queen with a good kicker (KQ or QJ), a smaller pair (JJ or TT) or two hearts for a flush draw.

The turn card is the Deuce of spades. The board is:

That card doesn't help Ronald, but it almost certainly did not help Brian. Ronald believes he has the best hand. He bets $250 into the $335 pot. Brian quickly calls. Ronald knows that with a set Brian would have raised by now. He would certainly fold a pair smaller than Queens. He might call with a Queen. But Ronald is convinced that Brian holds two hearts and is on a flush draw. Ronald will win the hand as long as the river card is not a heart.

The river card is the 7 of hearts. The board is:

Ronald's entire body deflates. Of all the rotten luck! If Brian was on a flush draw only nine of the remaining forty-four cards were hearts, leaving him barely a 20% chance of getting the card he needed. Yet there it is. Ronald checks. Brian stares at Ronald, then bets $475 into the $835 pot. Ronald believes the bet size is designed to entice him to call. It's the type of bet Brian would make with a flush. Ronald folds and shows his pocket Aces. Brian chuckles.

"You folded the best hand, Ron." He shows JT of clubs while raking in the chips. Ronald had been only half right. Brian was on a draw, but not a flush draw. He has bluffed Ronald out of the hand with a busted straight draw. His only chance was to get Ronald to fold. The bet was sized perfectly. If it was too small, Ronald would have called. He also would have called a large bet that looked like a bluff.

Ronald's face turns crimson. He feels a combination of rage and humiliation at being outplayed so badly. His mistake has cost him over $1300. Had he called Brian's bet he would be up almost $2000. After folding he's less than $700 ahead. He does not win another hand this night. When it comes time to cash in the chips, he is down almost $200. More than ever, he regrets his decision to allow Brian Ridge into the game.

As per custom, Brian is the first to leave at 11:15. He has won over $3000. As he drives out of the gated neighborhood, he feels vindicated that his superior play has again been rewarded. He does not see the rusting, red Jeep Cherokee parked in the shadows outside the gate. As he steers his Mercedes convertible onto I-75 South, he doesn't notice the same Jeep trailing him at a distance.

Brian almost always leaves the game early so he can get sufficient sleep before rising at 6:30 for his daily workout. It also leaves time for coitus, which makes it easier for him to get to sleep after playing poker. Among his phone contacts are a half-dozen women who have demonstrated willingness to meet him for a late-night rendezvous. It is a thirty-minute drive to his townhome in Hyde Park, so he is confident he'll find a taker. His first two text messages result in denials. His third choice is Jamie, a divorced nurse with a voracious sexual appetite. He did not try her first because, unlike the first two candidates, Jamie will insist on staying the entire night rather than leaving after one round. She responds within two minutes. She readily agrees to meet Brian at his townhome a few minutes after midnight.

At 11:50 Brian pulls into his driveway and remotely opens the garage door. He does not see the Jeep stop in front of an adjacent residence. Brian parks in the garage, turns off the ignition and steps out of his car. As he approaches the door leading into the home, someone in the garage says, "Don't turn around!"

Brian does not recognize the voice. He turns to see the outline of a tall man with a wiry build. Landscape lighting shines into the garage, preventing Brian from clearly seeing the man's face. As he steps closer, Brian can see that the intruder is wearing gloves and holding a pistol in his right hand. *This is not good,* Brian thinks.

The intruder extends his arm and points the gun directly at Brian. In a low voice he growls, "Turn around. Close the garage door and put your hands against that wall."

Brian does not panic. He presses a button and the garage door slowly, noisily lowers to the ground. The garage is dimly lit by an overhead light connected to the mechanism. Brian puts both hands against the back wall. While facing away from the intruder he says, "I've got about $8000 in my wallet. Just take it and go."

"Take your wallet out and toss it on the floor," responds the intruder. Brian complies. The intruder retrieves the wallet. After removing the cash and two credit cards he throws the wallet toward a side door. He asks, "Do you have an alarm system?" Brian, too terrified to speak, nods that he does.

"Is the alarm connected to that side door?" Brian nods again.

"Lie down in front of your car and start counting," the intruder commands. "Count slowly and don't stop until you get to a hundred."

Brian hesitates. Even with the garage door up he would not be visible from the street.

The intruder's voice becomes more insistent. "Face down! Do it!"

Brian reluctantly drops to the floor. He decides that the wisest course of action is not to resist.

"One, two…"

The intruder straddles Brian and puts the muzzle of the gun to the back of his head. He fires one shot. The sound reverberates within the enclosed space.

"You shouldn't have turned around."

The intruder presses the button to reopen the garage door. He walks quickly to the idling Jeep and climbs into the driver's seat. He puts the vehicle in gear and drives out of sight. Three minutes later the garage goes dark.

The Second Thursday

I T IS 8:46 ON THE MORNING of June 8th. Detective Andy Barlow stirs his second cup of coffee while leafing through a file. Born and raised in Colorado, Andy enlisted in the United States Marine Corps after graduating from high school. His twenty years of service included a tour of duty in Vietnam. During his military career he attended college classes and earned a degree in criminology. Following his discharge, he worked as an agent for the Drug Enforcement Administration for twenty years. With two federal pensions in hand, Andy and his wife decided to spend their remaining years in a warm climate. They moved to Tampa in 2009 after he was hired as a detective with the Tampa Police Department. For the past four years he had been in the homicide division. Last week he was assigned to investigate the robbery and murder of Brian Ridge.

Jamie Nelson called 9-1-1 during the early morning hours of June 2nd. She had arrived at Brian's residence a few minutes after midnight. As she parked in the driveway, she noticed that the garage door was raised and the garage was dark. She was puzzled because she had always entered Brian's townhome through the front door. Had he left the garage door open for her? Maybe he had taken his dog for a walk. Regardless, she decided to enter through the garage. As she approached the door leading into the home her right foot slipped across a wet spot. She fumbled to find a light switch. Turning on the overhead light, she saw a pool of blood extending to an area in front of Brian's car. She screamed when she saw Brian lying face down with a gaping wound in the back of his head.

Responding officers briefly interviewed Jamie and confirmed that Brian was deceased. They forced their way into the townhome, activating the security alarm in the process. An officer answered the telephone when a representative of the monitoring company called. The representative said the alarm had been set at 5:22 p.m. No zones were disturbed until the officers entered the residence. The only living being found during a sweep of the interior was a small, yapping dog in a crate. Officers established a perimeter with crime scene tape while awaiting the arrival of a homicide detective, a forensic technician and a representative from the medical examiner's office. Other officers conducted a neighborhood survey, asking people if they had seen or heard anything suspicious that night. Most of the neighbors had been sleeping. Some were irritated to be awakened at such an ungodly hour. Two who had been awake thought they heard a muffled bang around midnight. A few offered doorbell camera video.

An associate medical examiner arrived and conducted a preliminary examination of the body. There was an entrance wound to the back of the head and an exit wound above the left eye. The findings were consistent with a homicide caused by a single gunshot wound. Stippling around the entrance wound indicated the shot was fired at close range. The forensic technician found a 9-millimeter shell casing a few feet from Brian's head. A bullet fragment was partially imbedded in the concrete floor beneath him. Near the side door was a wallet containing Brian's identification, but no cash or credit cards. The technician dusted for fingerprints and was collecting blood and tissue samples when Detective Barlow arrived on scene.

Andy agreed with the assessment that a robbery and murder had occurred. The execution-style nature of the shooting made him wonder if Brian was targeted. He interviewed Jamie and quickly eliminated her as a suspect. She showed him the text messages that she and Brian had exchanged. His first message at 11:26 p.m. indicated he was on his way home after playing poker in Hunter's Green. She told Andy the only other player she knew was Cody King. She gave him Cody's cell phone number. She agreed to take Brian's dog until his family in Kansas could be notified. It was after 2 when Andy decided to call it a night.

Cody King arrived at school shortly after 8:30 that morning. The seniors had graduated the previous week and other students had completed final exams. For teachers it was the last day of work before the summer break. They had until the end of the day to turn in their grades and remove personal belongings from the classroom. Cody usually felt tired on mornings after poker, and that day was no exception. He had snorted cocaine before leaving the house in order to feel more alert. He planned to make it a short day.

Cody's cell phone rang shortly after 9. The display revealed an unfamiliar number, but he decided to answer it.

"Mr. King? This is Detective Barlow with the Tampa Police Department."

Cody gulped. Why was a police detective calling him?

Andy continued. "I want to ask you some questions about something that happened last night. How soon can you come downtown today and meet with me?"

"I guess I can come later this morning," Cody responded. "What's this about?"

"I'd rather not tell you over the phone. I'll fill you in when we talk. What time can you get here?"

"How about 11:30?"

Cody completed his tasks and arrived at the appointed time. He did not ingest any other substances that morning. He was wary even though he was no longer on probation. He knew he could not produce a clean urine sample. He became alarmed when he walked past Andy's office on their way to an interview room and saw that Andy was a homicide detective.

As soon as they sat, Cody asked, "What's this about?"

"We'll get to that in a minute. Where were you last night?"

Cody hesitated. He had hoped not to have to answer questions about drugs or gambling. On the other hand, if the police were investigating a murder a poker game would be a solid alibi.

"I was playing poker."

"Where?"

"At a house in Hunter's Green. A guy named Ron Turner hosts a game."

"How did you do?"

"I lost."

"How much?"

"About $2000."

"Wow! That's quite a game. Who else was there?" Cody listed the other players. Andy wrote each name on a yellow pad, carefully verifying the spelling.

"Who was the first to leave?"

"Brian left around 11:15, I think."

"Who left after Brian?"

"The rest of us stayed until the game broke at midnight."

"Why did Brian leave early?"

"He always leaves early. He gets up at 6 to work out."

"Did anyone call or text anybody after Brian left?"

"Not, not that I remember."

Andy noted that Cody seemed more nervous with each question. He decided to feel him out before telling him about Brian.

"How well do you know Brian?"

"We've been friends for about ten years. We play golf and poker together."

"Have you ever had any problems with him?"

Cody pondered the question. What did this guy know and what was he getting at?

"What kind of problems?"

"You tell me. Any kind."

"Just minor arguments and stuff, I guess."

"Did anybody have major problems with him?"

"Not that I know of."

"Do you know anybody who would want to kill him?"

Cody turned pale. "Why? Did somebody kill him?"

"Yes. He was murdered last night."

"Oh my God! What happened?" Cody seemed genuinely shocked.

"I can't give you any details yet. Can you think of anyone who might have wanted to kill him?"

"No! Nothing like that!"

Andy looked at Cody's arrest record. "I'm gonna check into the background of everyone at the game last night. I see you had a possession charge and a couple of DUIs. When was the last time you drank or used drugs?"

Cody felt as if Andy was staring right through him. How much should he tell?

"I drank some beer at poker last night. Do we really need to talk about drugs?"

"I just want to know if you're high right now. Do you understand my questions? Is your memory okay?"

"I'm fine."

"Anything else I should know? I'm not gonna jam you up on small stuff if it has nothing to do with the case."

Cody hesitated again. "I, I gamble sometimes."

"You mean besides poker?"

"Yeah. I bet on sports with a bookie."

"How do you do?"

"Usually not too bad. I've been losing lately."

"Do you owe any money?"

Cody paused. It was better left unsaid.

"Nah. I'm square."

Andy looked at his notes. He knew Cody was holding something back. Cody avoided eye contact and one leg was twitching.

"That's all the questions I have for now. I need the phone numbers of the other players from last night. Do me a favor and don't tell anyone about Brian until I've had a chance to talk to them."

One by one Dick, Matt, Robert, David and Scott arrived that afternoon to be interviewed. All expressed shock and denied knowledge of anyone who might want to kill Brian. Andy expected that. What he did not expect was the level of negative sentiment regarding Brian. They portrayed him as a manipulator who was often critical of the other players. Even more interesting, they identified Cody as the most frequent recipient of Brian's barbs.

Ronald was the last of the players to be interviewed. He arrived just after 4. As soon as he sat Andy said, "I want to ask you some questions about something that happened last night."

"Was Brian Ridge killed?"

Andy was caught off guard. "How did you know that?"

"I saw on the morning news that a man was murdered at his home in Hyde Park. After that I sent an email to count heads for next week's poker game. I heard back from everyone except Brian. Then I get a call from a homicide detective who wants to ask me some questions. It's not much of a stretch."

Andy thought Ronald seemed oddly unemotional about the situation. "What was Brian doing at your house last night?"

"Playing poker."

"What time did he leave?"

"About 11:15."

"Did you have any contact with him after that?"

"No."

"How about any of the other guys?"

"Not while we were playing. I can't speak for anybody after they left."

"What time did everyone else leave?"

"Just after midnight."

"How did Brian get along with the other players?"

"To be honest, nobody liked him too much."

"Why was that?"

Ronald told Andy about Brian's history with the game. Having played poker himself, Andy understood that most people would harbor some ill will about being hustled. Ronald kept talking.

"Cody was his best friend in the game but even he had some problems with Brian."

Andy perked up. "What kind of problems?"

"Brian was always ragging on him for being a bad player."

"Anything else?"

"No. That was pretty much it."

"How did you feel about Brian? You don't seem too broken up about this."

"Like I said, I figured it was him before I got here so I've had some time to process it. I'm sorry he's dead but he was not my favorite person. The atmosphere of the game is gonna be a lot better without him. Some of the guys wanted him out years ago."

"Was Cody one of them?"

"No. Brian brought Cody into the game. It was the other guys. For the last five years he took a lot of money from us that we'll never get back. And he was an asshole while doing it. One guy quit playing because of him."

"Who was that?"

"Jason Bowen."

"Can you give me Jason's phone number?"

"I guess. If that's all you need, I'd like to get out of here before the traffic gets any worse."

"What about the game? Will you guys take some time off?"

Ronald was perplexed. "I doubt it. We have alternates ready to go. Next man up. If the other guys are okay with it, we'll plug one in and get back to it next week."

Andy was taken aback. He flipped through his notes. "That's all for now."

Ronald gave Andy the phone number and left the station. While walking to his car he called Lisa to tell her about Brian.

Andy made a note that Ronald had identified two people who seemed to have a problem with Brian. He called Jason Bowen and scheduled an interview for Monday morning.

Following the autopsy, Brian's family arranged to have the body shipped to Kansas for a memorial service and burial. Ronald and the other players exchanged email messages that weekend. They arrived at two consensus decisions. The first was that all would contribute to the cost of a floral arrangement which Ronald would choose and send to the funeral home. The second was that the Thursday night games would continue uninterrupted. Russ Nichols was next in line to replace Brian as a regular.

At 9:30 Monday morning Jason Bowen arrived for his interview with Detective Barlow. He seemed defensive from the start.

"Why do you want to talk to me about this?"

"I understand you used to play poker with Brian."

"Yeah, so?"

"When was the last time you saw him?"

"The last time I played."

"When was that?"

"Three years ago."

"Why did you stop playing?"

"Because I was eighty years old and it was getting harder to win."

"Was Brian part of the reason?"

Jason pondered the question before answering. "Look, I was a consistent winner in that game for over twenty years. Then Brian weaseled his way in and I spent the next two years spinning my wheels. I just decided I'd had enough."

"Did you try to get him kicked out of the game?"

"Yes. Several of us told Ronald to get rid of him for the good of the game."

"But you were the only one who quit."

"Like I said, I was eighty years old and I'd had enough. But I don't know anything about who killed him. Wasn't it a robbery?"

"That's what I'm trying to find out."

"Well, I can't help you there. Are we done?"

Andy perused his notes.

"One more thing. Do you own a gun?"

"More than one. They haven't repealed the Second Amendment."

"How many do you have?"

"That's my personal business. They're all legal. Anything else?"

Andy stared at him for a moment.

"That's it for now."

Jason's aggravation grew as he walked to his car. The previous night he had told Ronald he was interested in returning to the game. He was disappointed to learn that Russ Nichols had already been chosen to fill Brian's spot. It was a bitter pill to be passed over for that ambulance chaser.

After Jason left the station, Andy reviewed additional evidence gathered over the weekend. Video from a doorbell camera showed an old SUV, probably a Jeep, pass in front of the home two doors down from Brian at 11:59 p.m. The license plate was not visible. On Saturday night a homeless man was arrested in East Tampa after trying to use Brian's Amex card to buy beer at a convenience store. He said he found the card on a sidewalk. Officers verified that at the time of Brian's murder the man was sleeping at a shelter. Why did the killer take the credit card only to discard it?

Andy viewed photographs of evidence from Brian's townhome. An entry scrawled on a notepad caught his eye.

Cody 100K 1ˢᵗ 10K due 6/15/17

Andy placed a call to Cody King. He had a few more questions.

Cody returned to the station that afternoon. Andy didn't mince words.

"I asked you before if you had any problems with Brian. Was there anything you didn't tell me?"

"No, not that I can think of."

"I'm told he liked to make fun of you for being a bad poker player."

"So? Brian needled everybody."

"Did it make you mad?"

"Sometimes, I guess. But not mad enough to kill him. Besides, I was still at Ron's house when it happened."

"I know that. Did you owe Brian any money?"

"N-no." Cody tried to sound convincing. He was never good at bluffing.

"I've got a piece of paper from his townhouse that says you owed him $100,000."

Cody nearly fell out of his chair before gathering himself.

"Should I talk to a lawyer?"

"That's up to you. A lawyer's gonna tell you not to talk to me anymore. If you didn't have anything to do with the murder this is probably your last chance to cooperate and get yourself clear. Otherwise, I'm gonna look hard at you and you might not like what I find. Would you rather come clean?"

Cody thought about it for a moment. "I'd better talk to a lawyer first."

Andy lowered his head, closed his eyes and sighed. "You're making it harder for both of us. You're free to go."

As soon as Cody got to the parking lot, he placed a call to Ronald Turner's brother Lee. Cody got Lee's card from Ronald after he was arrested for Possession of Cocaine and his second DUI in 2015. Lee managed to get the cocaine charge dismissed once Cody completed an outpatient treatment program. Cody pled guilty to DUI and was sentenced to a year of probation. Of course, he resumed drinking and using cocaine as soon as his probation ended. His license was suspended, with the exception of driving to and from work and appointments with doctors or lawyers. It was a big win to avoid jail time and a felony conviction.

Lee told Cody not to talk to anyone about the case and to come to his office at 9:30 the next morning.

Cody stayed up late that night. When his alarm sounded at 8:00 on Tuesday morning he turned it off rather than hit the snooze button. By the time Cindy awakened him it was 8:53. Cody rinsed off in the shower and threw on a pair of slacks and a knit shirt. Cindy poured him a cup of coffee. He inhaled the coffee, rushed out the door and jumped into his BMW 530i. He backed out of the driveway and drove one block to MacDill Avenue. He took a left on MacDill and a right on Kennedy Boulevard for the short trip to downtown Tampa. At least the morning rush hour traffic had mostly cleared. He parked in the garage of the building where Lee Turner's office was located.

When Cody stepped off the elevator on the 19th floor it was 9:42. Lee's receptionist checked him in and went to get him a cold bottle of water.

As soon as she returned with the water, Lee appeared and impatiently beckoned Cody into his office.

Lee looked ten years younger than Ronald, even though the age difference was less than two years. Compared to his older brother, Lee was two inches taller and twenty pounds lighter with a dark tan and a full head of brown hair. He wore a fitted, blue pinstripe suit with a Carlo Palazzi tie and black wingtips. Cody was suddenly conscious of how shabbily he was dressed. He knew his hair was unkempt. He sat timidly as Lee addressed him.

"I called Detective Barlow yesterday and told him that any further contact has to go through me. If he or anyone else calls you just tell them to call me. Say nothing else. Clear?"

"Clear."

"We've been through this before, so you know the drill. Everything you tell me is confidential."

"I understand."

"Okay. Now tell me how you came to borrow money from a dead guy."

"Well, he was alive when I borrowed it."

"That's a good start. Why did you need the money?"

"I owed it to a bookie. I had a bad run of betting on the playoffs."

"If we talk to the detective, we might leave that part out. How much did you owe?"

"About 80,000."

Lee whistled. "Was there any written record of that?"

"I didn't have one. I'm sure the bookie had something."

"How much did you borrow from Brian?"

"100 grand."

"When was that?"

"It was in two parts. The second was about ten days ago. I think it was the last Friday in May."

Lee looks at a Florida Gator desk calendar. "The 26th?"

"Sounds about right."

"Did you pay off the bookie? Do you still owe him anything?"

"No, I got square with him."

"Do you owe anybody other than Brian?"

"No."

"Did Brian keep a record of what you owed him?"

"I don't know but he must have. The detective said he knew about it from a piece of paper."

"What piece of paper?"

"Something they found in Brian's house."

"When did the detective interview you?"

"The first time was Friday."

"Did he ask about the loan then?"

"Not, not really."

"What does 'not really' mean? Either he did or he didn't."

"Well, he asked if I owed any money. I told him I didn't."

"That wasn't the smartest thing you could've said. When did you find out he knew?"

"He called me back yesterday and said he had some more questions. He asked if I owed Brian any money and I told him no."

"Why did you tell him that?"

"I didn't want him to think I had a reason to kill him."

"Great. By lying to him you made him think you might have had a reason. In the future, if you talk to the cops, it's better not to answer than to lie. I guess then he told you about the piece of paper."

"Right."

"And what did you tell him then?"

"I said I needed to talk to a lawyer."

"Good. That was smart. Is there anything you want to tell me about Brian getting killed.? Anything I need to know?"

Cody was taken aback. "No! I don't know anything about it!"

Lee raised his hands. "Hold on, I'm not accusing you. If there are any land mines out there, I just need to know where they are. We don't want to get blindsided again. So, no more surprises? You've told me everything I need to know?"

"That's it."

"Okay. Like I said, don't talk about this with anybody. That includes social media, Facebook, Twitter, what have you. If there's anything else, I'll be in touch."

"Got it."

Lee handed Cody a pen and a clipboard with an office form attached.

"This is the standard fee agreement, similar to the one you had two years ago. Look it over and let me know if you have any questions. If you're good with it, sign it and turn it in at the desk."

They both stood. Lee patted Cody on the back.

"It's gonna be okay."

It's almost 4 p.m. on Thursday the 8th. Lisa Turner is walking briskly through the physician parking lot at the Bay Pines VA Medical Center in Pinellas County. Her tour of duty ends at 4, but she left a little early today. She needs to get to the bank before the lobby closes at 5. If there are no unforeseen slowdowns, she should be home in time to have dinner with Ronald before he starts getting ready for poker. Public schools have let out for the summer and the snowbirds are gone, so rush hour traffic should be less odious than usual. Lisa climbs into her Audi Q7, pushes the ignition button and tunes the radio to a country music channel. She winds her way to I-275 North, then navigates the lanes of the Howard Frankland Bridge across Tampa Bay. The traffic flow is slower in the Westshore area. She makes a quick phone call as her progress slows to a crawl near downtown. After that, she thinks about the early days of her relationship with Ronald.

Lisa was in her third year of medical school when they met. Born in Atlanta in 1961, she was the youngest of four siblings. Both of her parents were architects. Lisa was the only one of the children who exceeded their parents' talent for precision. Any task she set out to accomplish was done in an orderly fashion. She detested dirt, germs and any other kind of mess. She grew to be accomplished, attractive and popular. She completed high school a year early and obtained an undergraduate degree in engineering from Georgia Tech University. During her senior year she decided that she wanted to be a physician. She was accepted to several medical schools. She opted to attend the University of Florida, largely because of fond memories of summer beach vacations her family took to places like Longboat Key and Sanibel Island. She began classes in September 1982. Only then did she realize that the campus in Gainesville was one of the few places on the peninsula that is ninety minutes from the nearest beach. During the first two years of didactic learning in basic sciences she ranked near the top of the class. The clinical rotations commenced in July 1984. After completing her rotation in internal medicine, she decided that she would become an infectious disease specialist. That discipline would be a natural fit for her germophobic nature.

In the spring of 1985 Lisa began her psychiatry rotation at Shands Hospital. Ronald was the resident assigned to supervise her and three other students. He was smitten from the start. His attraction to her was not reciprocated at first. She regarded Ronald as a nice, relatively bright guy who seemed nervous whenever they were alone. She had no interest in psychiatry, but he went out of his way to be helpful and patient with her. One morning during rounds she realized that the previous day she had forgotten to write a progress note on one of the patients assigned to her. The attending physician looked at the chart and observed that the note had been written by Ronald. He asked which medical student was assigned to the patient and why they had not written a note. Lisa prepared to confess and be reprimanded. Ronald spoke before she did.

"I told Lisa I'd write her last progress note if she would draw blood on Mr. Andrews."

The attending physician frowned and continued with rounds. Lisa and Ronald made eye contact. She realized why he had covered for her. On the last day of her rotation, she accepted his invitation to have dinner with him.

When Lisa and Ronald started dating, she did not foresee a long-term relationship. She had previously rejected marriage proposals from two men who did not meet her standards. Ronald fell short of her idealized mate in many areas, starting with his height. She had always preferred men over six feet tall, and Ronald was barely an inch taller than she was. She liked wearing heels and looked good in them. With Ronald, she thought, she'd have to give that up. His level of physical attractiveness was not comparable to hers. Her ideal man shared her interest in the humanities, whereas Ronald preferred watching sports. However, as the relationship progressed, she appreciated that he treated her with kindness and respect. She found herself feeling relaxed and secure when they were together. He could not match her level of cleanliness, but he did keep a tidier apartment than any of her previous boyfriends. He was willing to forego parenthood when she told him she didn't want children. He was not threatened by her desire to advance her career. In fact, he encouraged her. Although she would never tell him, what she counted on most was his devotion to her. *He's not someone who would cheat on me or leave me.* Following her medical school graduation in 1986, he proposed and she accepted.

For the next year, Ronald and Lisa lived together in an apartment in Gainesville. She began her residency program in internal medicine while he completed the fellowship in forensic psychiatry. She still had four years to go in her training. They made plans to be married in Atlanta when she was done. She encouraged Ronald to find a way to stay in Gainesville for a few years. She was disappointed when he declined an offer of a faculty position with the Department of Psychiatry. He wanted to enter private practice. Lisa wanted to live in Atlanta near her family after completing her training. She tried to convince Ronald to open a practice there. However, he was determined to return to Tampa to be near his own family. He established a practice in an office near USF and rented a nearby apartment. He lived in the apartment until he had the house in Hunter's Green built in 1990.

Lisa remained at UF to complete the additional years of training required to be an infectious disease specialist. She planned to join

Ronald in the new house once they were married. She did not expect to be offered her dream job: a position with the Centers for Disease Control in Atlanta. She tried again to convince Ronald to move to Atlanta. Again, he refused. She verbally accepted the position in the hope that he would change his mind. He did not. When the contract arrived in the mail, she reluctantly withdrew. She moved into the house in Hunter's Green after the wedding in 1991.

Lisa took a job on the staff of a VA facility close to their home. She soon learned that the medical staff was excellent and she enjoyed helping the veterans. However, she quickly became frustrated that time which should have been spent on patient care was wasted by relentless micromanagement and a stifling bureaucracy. After two years, she left to take a similar position at Bay Pines.

The drive from Hunter's Green to Bay Pines would be over an hour each way. Lisa reasoned that if she was going to work in Pinellas County, they might as well live at the beach. She tried to convince Ronald to buy a beachfront home and move his practice across the bay. He refused to consider it. His rationale was that he had spent six years establishing a practice in Tampa. They had a new house, built to his specifications. Ronald did not like change. He was adamant that Tampa was where he wanted to live and where he would practice. Lisa relented and prepared herself for long hours spent in her vehicle. She decided to embrace the house in Hunter's Green. She bought new furniture and decorated rooms to her taste. While she grew to love the neighborhood and the friends they made, she never relinquished her dream of a place on the beach.

When Ronald decided to retire in 2017, he encouraged Lisa to follow suit. She was eligible to take early retirement with generous pension benefits. Their retirement accounts were well funded. However, Lisa wanted both of them to work a few more years so they could afford a second home on the beach. Ronald vetoed the idea. He viewed a second home, especially one on the beach, as a financial albatross. He argued that they already had enough money to live comfortably in retirement. He wanted to travel and spend time with family and friends while they were still healthy and able.

It has been said that a man marries a woman and hopes she'll never change, while a woman marries a man hoping he will. After twenty-six years of marriage, Ronald had not changed. At first his consistency and reliability made Lisa feel safe. But after years of abandoning her own preferences, she had come to resent his rigidity. She knew marriage required compromise. After all, Ronald had agreed not to have kids. It wasn't until later that he revealed he was ambivalent about kids in the first place. Lisa had begun to question whether all her sacrifices had been worth it.

Ronald moved forward with his retirement plans. He cancelled his disability insurance policy. They agreed that they no longer needed life insurance and would not renew the policies when the premiums came due in July. Lisa elected to continue working. She hoped Ronald would soon become so bored he would at least find a part-time job and revisit the beach house idea.

Lisa emerges from the downtown bottleneck and heads east on I-4. The traffic is stop and go. She eventually reaches I-75 and proceeds north. For the remainder of the journey, she is able to drive at the speed limit. She exits at Bruce B. Downs Boulevard. She arrives at the bank with time to spare to conduct her business. From there it is a short drive to the house in Hunter's Green. Her Audi pulls into the garage at 5:21. She takes a deep breath before she gets out of the vehicle. Dinner conversation with Ronald on poker nights is never scintillating. He's usually distracted, rushing through the meal so he can get into the poker room by 6. She expects it to be more awkward than usual tonight. She typically has a glass of chardonnay with dinner. Tonight, one might not be enough.

At 5:40 Lisa and Ronald sit down to a meal of leftover chicken and yellow rice. The atmosphere is subdued. After a few minutes she asks, "Who is playing tonight?"

"The usual crew. Russ Nichols is replacing Brian."

Lisa shakes her head. "I don't know how you guys can do that. If one of my friends was murdered, I wouldn't be able to carry on the next week as if nothing had happened."

Ronald shrugs but does not respond. They finish eating in silence. Lisa and Sneakers go to the bedroom. After watching the evening news, Lisa will shower and change into pajamas. Ronald walks to the poker room to get ready.

Russ Nichols is the first to arrive. For three years he has bided his time as an alternate while eagerly awaiting the chance to become a regular. In a handful of previous sessions he had always lost, which he attributed to bad luck and his lack of familiarity with the other players. He believes he will do better as a regular.

Ronald greets him warmly, and why not? Russ is a likeable guy and an inept player with a lot of money. Ronald last saw him in March, when most of the players and their spouses gathered at Dick's house to watch the first Saturday of the NCAA basketball tournament. That day Russ brought Celeste, a young court reporter who was a former beauty pageant contestant.

Scott follows Russ into the room. He has come straight from his office. He removes his tie and shirt. He places the items in a small overnight bag. He removes a pajama top from the bag and slips it over his head. This is a ritual he performs whenever he has to work past 6. Ronald tolerates it, reasoning that Scott would be late for poker if he had to go home after work to change clothes.

"Is that a pajama top?" asks Russ. "This is why you guys can never play at my house. I'm trying to attract women, so I can't have people thinking I host slumber parties for middle-aged men."

Ronald and Scott laugh so hard they almost fall to the floor.

At 7:00 eight players are ready for the cards to be dealt. The atmosphere is surprisingly jovial. Little is said about Brian. Ronald and Cody are especially averse to the subject. Cody even sits in what used to be Brian's usual seat, believing it will bring him luck. He feels encouraged when he is dealt high card and gets the button for the first hand. He wins by raising pre-flop with AK. He's overdue for a night of good fortune. He decides now is the time to share the news about his pending fatherhood.

"Who has two thumbs and a pregnant wife?" Cody smiles and uses both thumbs to point to himself. "This guy."

"Congratulations," says Robert. "Who's the father?" Others express more congenial sentiments.

Matt deals the second hand. Scott and Ronald post the blinds. Dick and Robert fold. David raises to $30 as Ronald protests. "Stealing my blind already?" David just smiles. Russ folds while vowing to play tight tonight. Cody and Matt call. Scott and Ronald fold the blinds. The pot is $105. The flop is:

David quickly bets $75. Cody looks longingly at his cards before tossing them into the muck. "I guess I won't win every hand," he laments. Matt calls. The pot is $255.

The turn card is the 9 of hearts. The board is:

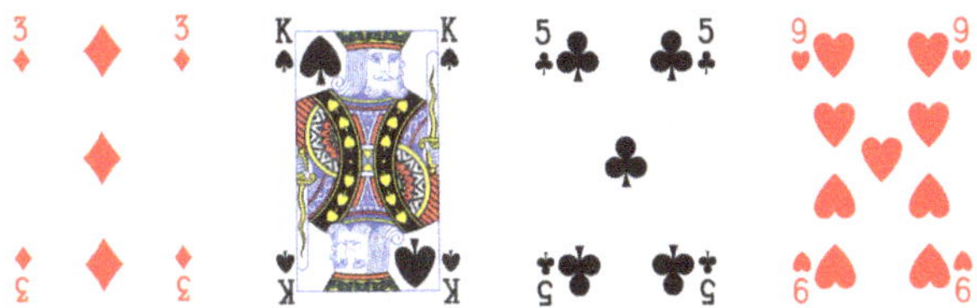

David bets $150. Matt quickly calls. The pot is now $555. David has $745 left. Matt has $740.

The river card is the 9 of spades. The board is:

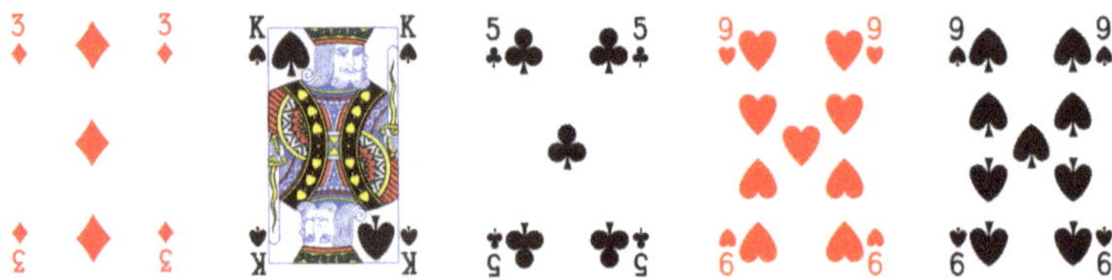

David thinks for a full minute, staring at Matt the whole time. He finally bets $200, barely a third of the pot. This is what's known as a blocking bet. A player acting first with a good but not great hand makes a small bet, hoping to preempt a large bet that would be difficult to call. Matt calls.

David shows KJ, giving him Kings and Nines with a Jack kicker. Matt shows KQ for Kings and Nines with a Queen kicker. Matt takes the $955 pot. David has already lost almost half his chips.

David lost the hand but his strategy with the blocking bet succeeded. Had he bet more, Matt probably would have called. Had he checked, Matt almost certainly would have bet $300 or more. David would have felt obligated to call rather than concede the pot with top pair and a good kicker. The bet saved him at least $100. This was an example of a hand played well by both players.

The conversation soon turns to the reality show in the White House. Earlier that day, James Comey told the Senate Intelligence Committee that the president had asked for his loyalty and pressured him to abandon the Russia investigation.

"The wheels are coming off," says Matt. "Flynn is long gone, the communications director resigned last week and now Sessions has offered to resign. It's only a matter of time."

"It's a witch hunt," says Cody. "It's all bogus."

Russ chimes in. "Add it up. Sessions didn't disclose two meetings with the Russian ambassador on his security clearance application. Jared tried to set up backchannel communication between the transition team and the Russians. Now Mueller's team is investigating Flynn and Manafort."

"So?" retorts Cody. "That doesn't mean Trump did anything wrong."

Ronald offers, "Steatorrhea won't be impeached no matter what Mueller digs up. Not with the Republicans in control of the House and the Senate."

"Wait until 2019," responds Robert. "The opposition party almost always gains seats in the mid-term election. If the Democrats get control, Pelosi will jump on him with both feet. It's not like she'll have to look hard to find something impeachable."

David speaks up. "What if she does? Even if he's impeached, they would need two-thirds of the Senate to convict. And even then I don't think he'd go anywhere. He'd declare martial law and rally his supporters. The deplorables would be marching in the streets."

Ronald nods. "Imagine the white trash riots. They might have to wait until he's out of office to prosecute him."

"Bill Cosby's trial started this week," notes Dick. "Maybe he and Trump can share a prison cell someday."

By 8:07 the hockey game has started. The Penguins score three first period goals on their way to a 6–0 win and a 3–2 series lead. Cody had bet $2000 on the Penguins to win tonight. It looks like things are finally turning in his favor.

It's Robert's turn to deal. David and Russ post the blinds. Cody limps from under the gun. Matt and Scott fold. Ronald calls with JT. Dick folds and Robert calls. David folds from the small blind. In the big blind Russ checks. Four players remain. The pot is $45. The flop is:

Ronald has flopped the nut straight. He starts thinking about what he'll do if Russ and Cody check. He could check to disguise the strength of his hand, hoping Robert bets after him or one of the others bets the turn. Another option is to bet a small amount to build the pot. He could even make a large bet to try to get heads up against a weaker hand. The decision becomes moot when Russ bets $40. Cody quickly calls. Ronald is delighted. He calls, hoping to string the two fish along. He is pleased when Robert also calls. The pot is $205.

The turn card is the 6 of clubs. The board is:

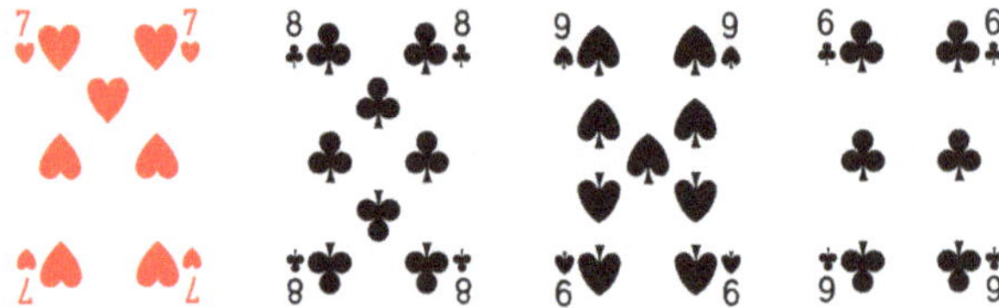

This is a great card for Ronald. Anyone holding a Five or a Ten has a smaller straight. Ronald's hand is still the nuts, but it is vulnerable with one card to come. If one of the other players has a set or two pair, they can make a full house if the board pairs. Anyone with two clubs can make a flush. A Ten or a Jack could give someone a bigger straight. As many as twenty-five cards could hurt him on the river.

Russ bets $150. Cody raises to $400. The pot has suddenly swelled to $755. Ronald has $905 in front of him. He knows he would kick himself if he played it slow and somebody caught him on the river.

"All in," he announces.

Robert grimaces. He looks at the board and at Ronald, going back and forth for over a minute. He counts everyone's chips. "All in," he says with resignation. Russ and Cody quickly call. The main pot is $3825, a teeming pile of red, blue, green and black chips. This hand will make someone's night and put three others in an early hole.

Russ and Cody both had $15 more than Ronald when the hand started. Robert had a little more than that. There is a side pot of

$45 consisting of the additional chips. The side pot is almost an afterthought.

Because there is no more betting, the players can show their hands before the last card is dealt. Russ has 87. He has been betting on his flopped two pair, but he needs an 8 or a 7 for a full house. Cody shows 96 of diamonds. Even suited, this is a weak hand to play from under the gun. He called after flopping top pair and a straight draw. He raised after turning two pair. He needs a 9 or a 6 for a full house. Both have badly overplayed their hand and made the pot much larger than it should have been. Robert is the innocent victim of their foolishness. He has QT of hearts, giving him a straight to the Ten. One of the three remaining Jacks would give him a higher straight than Ronald. No other river card can help him. No one is drawing to a flush. Ronald's straight to the Jack will hold up unless the board pairs or a Jack appears.

The river card is the King of diamonds. Robert's straight to the Ten wins the $45 side pot, which is small consolation. Ronald's straight to the Jack is good for the main pot. He embraces the chips as if he were hugging long lost friends. He's now up over $2800. By the end of the night he will have won almost $3500, his best game in years. He can't help but think about how the absence of Brian Ridge has made the game much more enjoyable.

Robert gives Russ and Cody a sideways glance as he collects the side pot. He is annoyed that they bloated the pot with what turned out to be the third and fourth best hands. He resists the urge to make a sarcastic comment. He reminds himself of the poker adage "Don't tap on the glass." In other words, you don't want to scare the fish. Robert, Russ and Cody buy more chips. Robert will exact retribution later.

"It'll be a double whammy if I lose tonight," says Russ. "I passed up a chance to get laid."

"Are you still seeing Celeste?" asks Dick.

"Nah, I broke it off a few weeks ago."

Matt is flabbergasted.

"What could possibly make you decide you didn't want to hit that anymore?"

Russ shrugs. "No matter how hot she is, sooner or later you get tired of her shit."

At 9:13 a more typical hand takes place. Scott is on the button. Ronald and Dick post the blinds. Robert and David fold. Russ and Cody call, as usual. Matt folds. Scott looks down at JJ and raises to $40. Ronald folds from the small blind. Dick, in the big blind, looks down at 99. He calls the additional $30. Russ calls with who knows what. Cody reluctantly folds.

Ronald, as if channeling Brian, needles Cody. "That hand must have been garbage." Other players chuckle.

The pot is $135. The flop is:

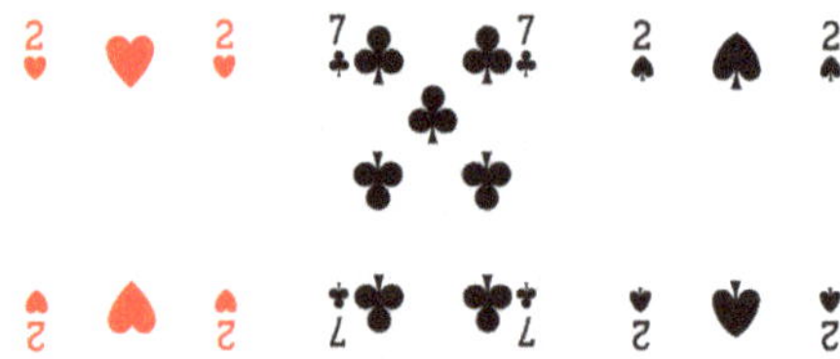

Both Dick and Scott are pleased with this flop. None of the cards on the board are higher than their pocket pairs. Dick and Russ check. Scott bets $100. Dick quickly calls. Russ sighs and tosses his cards into the muck. "I can't catch a break tonight," he laments. The pot is $335.

The turn card is the Ace of diamonds. The board is:

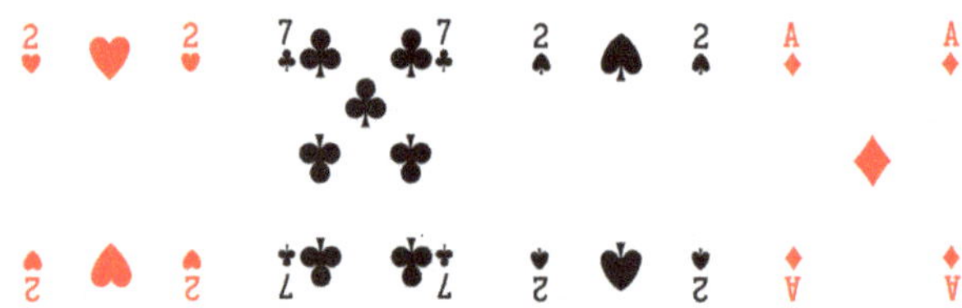

This is what's known as a scare card. Both players must be concerned that the other has a hand like AQ or AJ, in which case they would have paired their Ace. Any bet is likely to be called only by someone with an Ace.

Both players check. The river card is a 5. The board is:

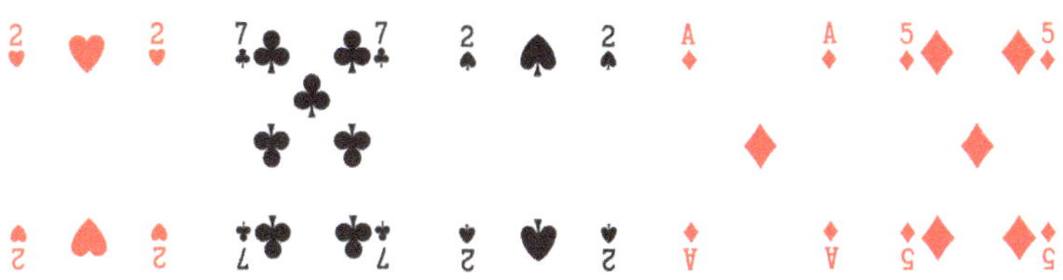

Dick eyes Scott, then bets $200. Scott returns the stare, then calls. Scott's Jacks and Deuces are good, and he takes the substantial pot. Another unremarkable hand well played by both.

At 9:45 Scott suddenly realizes that Cody didn't ride to the game with Brian.

"Cody, how'd you get here tonight?"

"Uber. If I'm gonna pay for rides both ways, I'd better turn this night around. At this rate I'll be hitchhiking."

Dick deals the cards. Robert and David post the blinds. Russ and Cody limp. Matt folds. Scott looks down at K9, a marginal hand. But Scott is two seats off the button, also known as the hijack seat. When no players raise in front of him, a player in this position will sometimes raise in an effort to hijack the button. If the next two players fold, the player in the hijack seat will have position for the rest of the hand. If everyone folds, he has stolen the pot. Scott raises to $35.

Ronald, in the cutoff seat, looks down at QJ suited. Ordinarily, this hand is not good enough to call a raise. But he knows that Scott might be raising with a marginal hand. And Ronald will have position. He calls, thwarting Scott's hijack plan.

Dick folds from the button. Robert folds from the small blind. David, in the big blind, looks down at 72. This is usually considered the worst starting hand in Hold 'Em. An easy fold.

David raises to $100.

Russ and Cody quickly fold. Back to Scott, who sheepishly grins like a thief caught red-handed. He folds. It's up to Ronald. Ronald eyes David with suspicion while considering his options. He could call and play the hand in position, or even raise to find out if David has a real hand. But he decides not to risk ruining a good night by playing a big pot with QJ. His cards find the muck. David collects the pot, of which $85 is profit.

David has successfully executed a squeeze play. He knew that Scott might be raising with a less than premium hand from the hijack seat. He was gambling that Scott did not have a monster like AA or KK. He knew that Ronald would have raised Scott if he had a big hand, so he was unlikely to call a raise to $100. The gamble paid off.

At 10:17 it's Ronald's turn to deal. Dick and Robert are the blinds. David folds. Russ limps with Q9. Cody calls with 63. Matt calls with KJ. Scott and Ronald fold. Dick folds from the small blind. Robert checks from the big blind with 54. His patience is about to be rewarded. The pot is $45. The flop is:

There is something in this flop for everybody except Matt. Robert has an open-end straight draw. He checks. Russ bets $25 with top pair. Cody has bottom two pair. He raises to $60. Matt folds. Robert and Russ call. The pot is $225.

The Deuce that hits the turn is decisive. The board is:

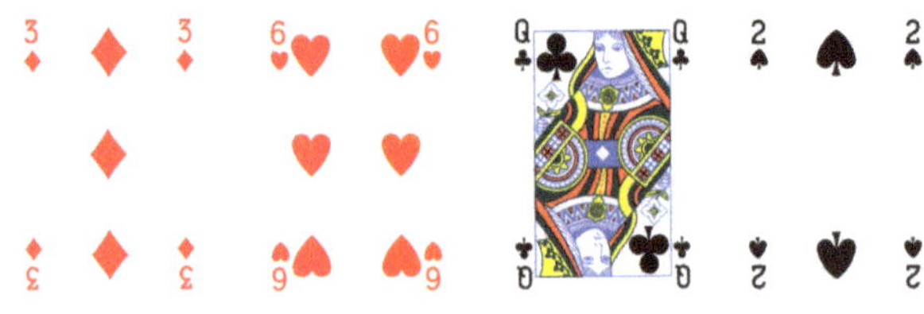

For Robert it is the dream card. His 54 makes a straight for the nuts. He checks, as does Russ. Cody bets $150 with his two pair. Back to Robert, who seizes the opportunity to put the hammer down. He check-raises to $400. Russ should fold but he calls, drawing dead. Cody calls as well. He needs a 6 or a 3 for a full house. The pot is $1425. Russ and Cody have a little over $500 left. Robert has both of them covered, meaning he has more.

The river card is a Jack, which changes nothing. Robert moves all in. Russ ponders for a moment, then calls. Cody quickly calls as Russ groans. Robert is ecstatic. The pot is almost $3000.

"I've got the nuts," proclaims Robert as they show their cards. He gathers the pot as Cody grouses that he thought his two pair was good. Russ chimes in. "I should have known top pair was no good. With a pot that big I couldn't lay it down." He and Cody buy more chips, ammunition each will use to shoot himself in the foot.

Russ loses the last of his chips at 11:19. He is down $3000. He opens his wallet and removes the four remaining bills, all singles. He decides to call it a night rather than ask Ronald for chips on credit to play another forty minutes. He resists the impulse to slam the front door on his way out of the house. Ronald had warned all players that they risked the wrath of Lisa should any noise be loud enough to awaken her. Russ starts his Jaguar XJR, drives one block and waits for the exit gate to open.

A rusting, red Jeep Cherokee pulls alongside the keypad in front of the entrance gate at 11:28. The driver presses a sequence of numbers to open the gate. Nothing happens. He tries the same numbers again with the same result. He struggles to remember if he needs to press the * key before or after entering the numbers. He then sees the Jaguar rolling through the exit. He makes a U-turn and follows the vehicle.

Russ drives to his house in South Tampa, arriving five minutes before midnight. He parks the Jaguar in the cluttered garage. The Jeep stops in front of the house next door, the motor still running. The driver steps out of the vehicle. His name is Lucas. He is tall and thin, with a scraggly beard and a jagged scar across his left cheek. His thinning hair is pulled back into a ponytail. He's wearing a tank top, revealing a neck and arms covered with tattoos. He slips on a pair of gloves and a ski mask.

Russ walks to the door and presses a button to close the garage door. The garage door lowers a few feet but abruptly halts as the sensor detects Lucas entering the garage. Lucas points a Taurus 9-millimeter pistol at Russ.

"Close the garage door," he orders.

Russ immediately thinks of Brian Ridge. He fumbles for his house key. Gun still extended, Lucas moves around the passenger side of the Jaguar toward Russ and the door leading into the house. Russ ducks behind the hood of the car. He has to think of a way to get the intruder away from the door.

Lucas stands in front of the door. "I don't want to shoot you," he says. "I just want your money."

Russ doesn't believe him. He decides his best chance is to run through the garage door opening and yell for help. He moves to the driver side of the Jaguar and looks for a way to distract the intruder. He sees his golf bag and grabs an iron from it. He stands and flings the club at Lucas. Lucas ducks as the club crashes into the wall behind him. Russ grabs another iron and makes a dash for the opening. As he ducks under the garage door, he hears the unmistakable sound of a gunshot. The slug rips into the back of his left thigh. Russ tumbles onto the driveway, iron still in hand.

Lucas moves swiftly to where Russ lies writhing in pain. Lucas stands over him, points the gun and hisses, "Don't make me kill you. Give up your wallet."

Russ is determined not to go down without a fight. He grips the iron and swings it with all the strength he can muster. The club face makes solid contact with the assailant's left knee.

In the next two seconds, Lucas does three things. He screams an obscenity. He grabs his left knee with his left hand. Then, he shoots Russ in the throat.

Russ drops the iron and holds both hands over his throat. Blood spurts between his fingers. He goes limp and does not move or speak again. Lucas bends his right knee to the ground, rolls Russ onto his left side and removes a wallet from the right back pocket. He opens the wallet and sees $4. He frantically searches other pockets but finds only a set of keys. He glances around the neighborhood. Several previously dark houses are now illuminated. Lucas takes the wallet, runs to the Jeep and speeds out of the neighborhood.

The Third Thursday

IT IS JUNE 15TH. Ronald Turner awakens to the sound of his alarm clock at 7:45. He sits on the edge of the bed. What will he do today? He had looked forward to retirement and never thought he would have difficulty filling his days. He liked the idea that he could read, watch a movie or go to the gym with no time pressure. After six weeks, though, he found himself getting easily bored. More than ever, he looked forward to the Thursday night poker games. However, following the murder of Russ Nichols, he and the other players agreed to heed Detective Barlow's admonition to put the game on hold until the killer could be apprehended.

The evening after Russ was murdered, Lisa told Ronald, "We need to get a gun."

Ronald was reluctant. "Why? So I can shoot myself while cleaning it? That's what would happen to me. I've never touched a gun, and neither have you. People like us are safer without them."

"Ordinarily I would agree with you, but there's nothing ordinary about this. Somebody's after you guys. If Russ had a gun instead of a golf club, he might still be alive."

"Maybe, but why do you think we need to be worried? If anybody needs to protect themselves, it's the guys in South Tampa. Both of the murders happened there. What makes you think the killer would come all the way out here?"

Lisa raised her voice. "Both of those guys had just left YOUR poker game! Do you think it's a coincidence? They were the first guys to leave! Maybe he followed them!"

"If he's waiting for guys to leave the poker game, he's gonna have a long wait. We're not playing again until he's caught."

"If he knows about the game he might know where we live. What if he comes here next? Do you really want to take that chance?"

Ronald closed his eyes and sighed. "Don't we have enough protection? We live in a gated neighborhood. We have security alarms and cameras. All the doors have deadbolts. The windows are shatterproof glass. This place is practically a fortress. If the guy can get through all that, how are we gonna stop him with a gun we have locked away somewhere?"

Lisa was undeterred. "If he gets into the house, I want something we can use to protect ourselves."

"Maybe you can sic your cat on him."

Lisa was not amused. Ronald knew it was time to surrender.

"Okay. A gun it is."

The next day they bought a .38 caliber Ruger LCR and two boxes of ammunition from Ronald's cousin. They made plans to go to a firing range the following Saturday.

At 7:48 Ronald is still sitting on the edge of the bed. He briefly considers taking the gun to the range to get a head start. He decides to wait until Saturday when Lisa can go with him. He thinks about spending the afternoon at the Seminole Hard Rock Casino poker room, but quickly rejects the idea. Playing with strangers wasn't nearly as much fun as playing with friends in the weekly home game. He had done pretty well playing 1-2 and 2-5 No Limit at the Hard Rock, but the stakes were not high enough to hold his interest. He was a big loser the last three times he played 5-10. And when he came home his clothes smelled like smoke.

As Ronald pours a bowl of Cheerios, he thinks about what he will do for lunch. He and Jason Bowen used to have lunch almost every Thursday, but the tradition fell by the wayside when Jason dropped out of the Thursday night game. Jason called again last weekend. He told Ronald he didn't want to seem like a vulture, but he was calling dibs on the seat vacated by Russ. He said he missed the game, at least the one that did not include Brian Ridge. Ronald told him the game was on hiatus until the killer was apprehended. He added that when they were cleared to resume playing, the regulars would vote on who should fill the seat. Ronald said he would recommend Jason, but he couldn't promise anything. Jason was disappointed and wondered aloud how anyone could have priority over him. Secretly, Ronald would prefer that the seat be filled by a player who was not as good as Jason. Ronald knows Jason suspects as much. He doesn't want Jason to think he's trying to keep him out of the game. He decides to call him later and see if he's free for lunch.

Andy Barlow sits at his desk at 8:49. By now he has almost memorized the files pertaining to the murders of Brian Ridge and Russ Nichols. It has been a week since he received the late-night call about Russ. As he drove to the scene, he couldn't help but think about Bill Murray in *Groundhog Day*. He arrived to find Russ lying supine on the driveway. There was a 6-iron to the right of him and a 9-millimeter shell casing on his left. A gunshot wound to the throat was the obvious cause of death. He also had a wound of the left posterior thigh. In the garage was a 5-iron and a similar shell casing. There was blood on the driveway between Russ and the garage. It was apparent to Andy that the assailant ambushed Russ in the garage. Russ probably used the golf clubs to fight back. He attempted to escape under the garage door but was stopped when he was shot in the thigh. The shot to the throat finished him.

Several neighbors heard two shots about fifteen seconds apart. A man walking his dog saw a white male leave the scene in an old-model red Jeep Cherokee. Two doorbell cameras caught the vehicle on video. Still no license plate.

The next afternoon, Lisa Turner and one of the other poker wives called Andy to ask if a patrol car could be parked in front of their houses at night. Andy told them that was not feasible. He said he could get a marked unit to drive by the houses every hour or so. He also offered to facilitate if they wanted to hire off-duty officers as private security guards.

 Andy studies the files again. *What's the connection to the poker game? Is somebody stalking the players?* The assailant was not one of them, but somebody could be feeding him information. Andy had conducted another round of interviews of the players. All but one of the surviving participants of last week's game had cooperated. Andy contacted Lee Turner about Cody King, but Lee denied the interview request. Andy also asked Jason Bowen to return for a second interview. Jason declined. After the first round of interviews, Andy had noted both Ronald and Jason were anxious to get out of Dodge. Neither of them seemed very sorry about Brian. Both gave Andy an uneasy feeling, but are they killers? Cody had a potential motive to kill Brian. But why would he kill Russ? According to the other players, Cody and Russ were friends. In fact, none of them seemed to harbor ill feelings toward Russ. That was in stark contrast to the way they talked about Brian.

Cody arrives at the country club for his 9:05 tee time. Ever since he started teaching, he has made a habit of playing golf three or four times a week while on summer break. He liked starting in the morning to get the jump on Tampa's heat and humidity. For the past ten years he had usually played with Brian. They were a good match when it came to golf. They both played fast. They both liked to bet, usually $100 a hole. Their handicaps were similar, so most of the rounds were close and the wagering usually evened out. They enjoyed each other's company, at least when they weren't talking about poker. They often mixed jokes with constructive comments about each other's game.

Today Cody is partnered with Mark West, a friend from high school who happened to be available. Unlike Brian, Mark is a slow player, has no sense of humor and does not like to bet. The lack of gambling isn't a dealbreaker, but a four-hour round with a boring player could prove to be a grind.

Everything is okay for the first few holes. Cody gets off to a great start with three pars and a birdie. He is on his game and starts thinking he could challenge his personal best of 73. Mark is not playing as well or as fast, but it's not much of a problem until the fifth hole. Mark slices his tee shot into heavy woods to the right of the fairway. The area is overgrown and saturated from early summer thunderstorms. Finding the ball would be like finding a needle in a soggy haystack. Instead of taking a drop, he insists on taking time to search. He looks for at least five minutes, maybe closer to ten. Cody hits his second shot, then sits in the cart and stews. Finally, Mark gives up and decides to take the drop after all. Cody is frustrated to the point that he loses concentration on the green, resulting in his first bogey.

Hole by hole, Cody's focus shifts from his game to how slowly Mark is playing. Mark doesn't waste much time off the tee, but things slow to a crawl from there. He methodically considers the yardage, the wind and the slope before choosing his club for every approach shot. Then he takes forever over the ball. Almost every hole, Cody finds himself muttering, "Just hit the damn ball, already." When Mark goes to chip he doesn't bring his putter, so after the shot he has to walk back to the cart to make the exchange. While lining up a putt he looks at every possible angle, as if he were on the PGA tour. Then he hits a piss-poor putt and has to do it all again. After every hole he stands on the green to write down his score, rather than doing it while waiting at the next tee. Being deliberate does not help his game.

Meanwhile, Cody's game deteriorates. When it comes to golf, stress is not an ingredient of the recipe for success or fun. He finishes the front nine with a 38 after three more bogeys.

Ronald calls Jason just before 11. Jason is getting ready to leave the headquarters of the Hillsborough County Republican Party. He has had a productive morning. He garnered over $9000 in pledges for the campaign to "Stop the witch hunt." He looks at his caller ID and answers.

"Hello, Ronald. How can I help you, sir?"

"Are you free for lunch?"

"Today is your lucky day. I am available."

"Where would you like me to pick you up?"

"I'm going home now. You can pick me up at 11:30." Jason knows better than to offer to drive. After several near misses, Ronald vowed never again to get into a car with Jason behind the wheel.

Jason is standing in front of his townhome when Ronald arrives in his Honda Accord. Ronald stops and unlocks the doors. Jason climbs into the front passenger seat as Ronald greets him.

"Good to see you, Jason. How about First Watch?"

"Sounds good. How was San Diego? Did Lisa go with you?"

"No. She didn't want to take the time away from work. She's been there twice for meetings of her own. And she's never liked hanging out with a bunch of psychiatrists."

"Why not?"

"Too many nerds who give her the creeps. It was just as well. It gave me a chance to catch up with people I might not see again."

"So, you were a bachelor on the road. What kind of trouble did you get into?"

The question catches Ronald off guard. He struggles to answer casually.

"None, none. Went to lectures, dinner, the zoo. That's about it."

Ronald is not telling the whole truth. He flew out on Friday the 19th and checked into the Marriott Marquis near the convention center. That night he had dinner with a former medical school classmate. On Saturday he took a shuttle bus to the zoo and spent most of the day there. He then went to dinner with two psychiatrists he knew from his residency program. He spent most of Sunday hanging around the convention center, ducking in and out of lectures while catching up with other old friends. At 5:30 he was preparing to walk back to the hotel when he saw Shana Parker standing near an exit.

Shana grew up in Fort Lauderdale. She was always the prettiest girl in class. In high school she was voted homecoming queen. She attended Florida State University, majoring in broadcast journalism after an academic adviser told her she had a face for television. After graduation she took a job as a reporter for Channel 13 in Tampa. Five feet five inches, brunette and curvaceous, she was declared the winner of several unofficial polls to determine the hottest woman on TV in the Tampa area. She became a favorite of the male audience, Ronald included. She interviewed him in 1997 after he testified in a high-profile murder trial. He marveled that she was even more attractive in person than on television.

In 1998 Shana was still a field reporter. She sometimes filled in for anchors on weekends. Her goal was to become the station's lead female anchor. However, Kelly Ring was firmly entrenched in that position and seemed unlikely to relinquish it anytime soon. Shana realized that if she stayed at Channel 13 her opportunities for advancement were limited. She decided she needed a fresh start somewhere else. She accepted a job at the CBS affiliate in San Diego, a larger market. She would begin as a field reporter with the opportunity to earn a promotion to anchor. In 1999 she met and married Ricky Vee, a popular DJ of a local radio station. Over the next few years they bought a house, adopted two young boys and settled into what appeared to be the ideal life of a local power couple.

By 2017 Shana viewed her life as a series of disappointments. After nineteen years at the station, she was still a field reporter. She was usually assigned fluff pieces rather than hard news. The main reason was her tendency to flub lines during live shots. She also believed that while her looks had opened doors for her, they also prevented some in the industry from taking her more seriously. At forty-six she was still attractive, but no longer the shiniest model on the showroom floor. Over the last two years her family had splintered. Her older son was attending a university in the northern part of the state and rarely came home. Her younger son had behavioral problems and was attending a residential school in Arizona. Her marriage had failed. There were problems early in the relationship due to Ricky's infidelity, but she tried to forgive him as they attempted to provide a stable home for their sons. Shana thought things were fine until 2016, when Ricky left her for a thirty-year-old producer at the radio station. They sold the marital home. Shana moved into the nicest one-bedroom apartment she could afford near downtown. She had few female friends and rarely socialized. She had been asked on several dates since the separation but had declined, not wanting to put her heart at further risk. The divorce was finalized two days before she ran into Ronald Turner.

Shana was assigned to report on the event that afternoon. She had finished recording a segment to air on the 6 p.m. newscast. Her cameraman was on the way back to the station and she was done for the day. Monday and Tuesday were her days off. She was planning to drive to her apartment, have a glass of wine and eat dinner in front of the TV while watching *60 Minutes*. Ronald approached her just before she reached the exit. She vaguely remembered him from the time she interviewed him in Tampa. On that occasion he had been unable to hide his crush on her. She rewarded him with girlish flirting, as she often did with male interview subjects. She saw no harm in stroking the ego of a man in whom she had no interest and never expected to see again. She reasoned that boosting the subject's confidence often resulted in a better interview.

As she stood talking to Ronald at the convention center, Shana could see that he was still infatuated. She was wearing a tight skirt and a scoop neck top, similar to the attire that had been her trademark at Channel 13. In his eyes she was still the twenty-six-year-old rising star who had interviewed him, not the divorcee with estranged children and a stalled career, twenty years older and ten pounds heavier. She found herself enjoying the company of this man who flattered her and reminded her of a more promising time in her life. He wore a wedding ring and mentioned that his wife was a doctor at the Bay Pines VA. No matter. In that moment, spending time with him seemed more appealing than dining alone in her apartment. She told him she had made dinner plans, but her friend had cancelled. She asked Ronald if he would join her so she could catch up on what was happening in Tampa. He readily accepted, truthfully saying he was free. She excused herself to find a restroom. She used the opportunity to make a 6:30 reservation at Lou & Mickey's, a steakhouse across the road from the convention center.

While Shana was gone, Ronald called Lisa to tell her he was having dinner with friends and would be out late. Lisa was getting ready for bed and did not ask questions. He told her he had seen Shana Parker covering the event and had said hello. Lisa used to refer to Shana as Ronald's TV girlfriend. Had she ever granted him a hall pass, she knew Shana would be near the top of his list. She teased that he'd better leave her alone or Shana might report him for stalking. He told her that Shana had left for the day and was not coming back.

When Shana returned, she asked Ronald for a favor. She was carrying a large backpack, which contained a small purse as well as personal items she used during the day. She said the backpack was heavy and she didn't want to carry it across the street and into the restaurant. Ronald offered to carry it for her. Shana asked if she could leave the backpack in Ronald's hotel room, which was on the way to the garage where her car was parked. That way, she could take only her purse to dinner. After dinner it would be easy to retrieve the backpack before going to her car. Ronald agreed. After depositing the backpack in the room, they walked to the restaurant. It seemed like a dream to Ronald. After Shana left Channel 13 he never expected to see her on TV again, much less have dinner with her. Not to mention a required return to his hotel room.

Ronald had two bottles of beer with dinner. Shana had three glasses of wine. Both ordered filet mignon. They talked about Tampa politics, the lack of mass transit, the development of the Channelside District, the demise of the *Tampa Tribune,* the move of the medical school, the enduring excellence of Bern's Steak House and the Columbia Restaurant, the Rays' stadium conundrum and the championships won by the Bucs and the Bolts. Shana expressed regret that San Diego would lose the Chargers without seeing them win a Super Bowl. She said little about the dissolution of her marriage or her dissatisfaction with her career. She did confess that after all those years of living in a house with a husband and children, it was sometimes hard to go home to an empty apartment. Ronald commended her patience in tolerating an autograph seeker and two others who asked her to pose for pictures. By the time the check arrived she had become more gregarious and flirtatious. She offered to pay but he insisted they divide it.

Ronald and Shana walked back to the hotel. She held onto his arm, which she said was necessary to navigate the walkway in heels after drinking wine. *God, she smelled good.* He realized the best he could do was chew on a mint and hope that his morning shower and deodorant were holding up. He could not help but wonder about her intentions. Inviting him to dinner was one thing. Leaving her bag in his room was another. Was it an excuse for her to return to the room? If so, did she just want to talk or did she have something else in mind? The room had one bed. If she was too impaired to drive, should he invite her to stay or help her get a cab? The last thing he wanted to do was read too much into her actions. He resolved not to ruin the memory of a nice evening by ending it with an unwelcome sexual advance. If anything was going to happen, she would have to take the lead.

Ronald had never cheated on Lisa. But if presented the opportunity to bed Shana Parker, he did not think his marriage vows would be a match for the desire to fulfill a long-held fantasy. He felt excited and nervous at the prospect of such a dilemma.

They rode up the elevator with two other couples returning from dinner. Still holding Ronald's arm, Shana kissed him on the neck before resting her head on his shoulder. He was unsure how to interpret these gestures, affectionate but not necessarily sexual. All doubt was removed once he closed the door to the room. She began kissing him on the lips, gently at first, then more urgently. He briefly hesitated but did not resist. She unzipped his fly and fondled him, a step she could have easily skipped. The last time his penis got erect so quickly was the night of his high school prom. He knew he'd feel guilty later, but he might as well enjoy what was happening. He went deep into his memory to recall what used to pass for moves. They made their way onto the bed. Ronald was never adept at dirty talk, so he elected not to speak. As he undressed her, he felt like he was in a late-night Cinemax movie. He verified that the breasts he had ogled were not surgically enhanced.

Fifty minutes later Ronald finished for the second time. The first did not take long and the recovery period was substantial. He had more stamina the second time, but she was less enthusiastic and no more satisfied. She did not pretend to climax, and he did not bother asking. She was quiet afterward. Shortly before 10 she rose to get dressed. She said she wanted to sleep in her own bed. He was simultaneously disappointed and relieved. He offered to walk her to her car, but she declined. She said she wanted to get some air and clear her head before driving home. He put on his pants, and they stood awkwardly at the door. Neither of them asked for the other's contact information. She kissed him on the cheek, opened the door and allowed it to shut behind her.

The bittersweet nature of the memory snaps Ronald back to reality. A wave of guilt washes over him as he parks in front of the restaurant. He imagines confessing to Lisa and asking for forgiveness, then thinks better of it. *I need to take this to my grave.*

There is no wait. Ronald and Jason are escorted to a booth near the front window. The waitress pours them each a glass of water. She offers them menus, but they're both ready to order.

The food arrives in less than ten minutes. Jason cuts and mixes his grilled chicken Caesar salad. Ronald takes a bite of his turkey burger as Jason resumes talking.

"So, how soon do you think we can resume playing?"

Ronald finishes chewing his food. He knew the question would come sooner or later.

"Still no word. The detective doesn't think it's safe until they catch the guy."

"How close do you think they are?"

"No idea. The detective interviewed me again Monday, but he didn't tell me anything I didn't already know."

"He called and asked me to go down there again. I told him to forget it."

Ronald is perplexed.

"Why wouldn't you go?"

Jason scowls.

"I don't have anything to tell him. He's wasted enough of my time. I don't have that much time left, you know."

Ronald smiles but doesn't answer. Jason enjoys telling that joke.

"Have you asked the guys whether they're okay with me coming back?"

"We haven't talked about it."

"You don't see a problem, do you?"

"It's not up to me. And technically, Bill Mumphrey is next on the list."

"But you can veto somebody if you want. It's your house."

Ronald can see that Jason won't let this go unless he gives him something.

"When the time comes, I'll push for you. That's all I can promise."

Jason isn't satisfied, but he can see that will have to do. They move on to other topics.

The back nine is no more enjoyable for Cody. He gathers himself to make par on the tenth and eleventh holes. He hits a good tee shot on the twelfth, a par 4. He estimates the approach to be 160 yards. He chooses a 7-iron and steps over the ball. Mark, who should be preparing for his next shot, decides it's time to impart some of his wisdom.

"I think you need more club. The pin is at the back of the green."

Cody steps back and nods, but he resents the unsolicited advice. If he uses too much club he could go over the green, leaving himself short-sided coming back. Jack Nicklaus always preached the opposite. Since perfect shots are rare, rather than invite trouble you should aim for the middle of the green. That way, you can salvage par even if you hit a mediocre shot. This pin placement calls for less club.

Cody resumes his stance over the ball. Mark sees that his suggestion won't be heeded.

"Your funeral."

As Cody swings, Mark's words echo in his head. He hits as much grass as ball, sending a divot almost ten feet. The ball lands in the rough, short of the green. Mark chuckles.

"Can't say I didn't warn you."

Cody walks dejectedly to the cart. He does not look at Mark. On this hole he will make the first of four consecutive bogeys. What started as a promising round has turned to shit.

Ronald drops Jason at his townhome shortly after 1. He needs to pick up a few things at Publix on the way home. He decides to get some flowers for Lisa while there. He feels the need to earn some points, even if she doesn't know why. He pulls into the parking lot and finds a spot next to a tree. After gathering his list, coupons and reusable bags he walks into the store.

Ronald wipes down a cart and heads to the produce section. While looking at bananas he hears someone behind him say in a sharp voice, "Hey! Turner!"

Ronald turns to see a tall, thin, unkempt white male who looks to be in his thirties. Ronald doesn't recognize him. He eyes the stranger warily.

"Do I know you, sir?"

"You took three years from me. I ought to kick your ass."

Ronald's heart starts racing. *Is this the guy? Am I next?*

"I, I'm sorry but I don't know what you mean."

"I'm gonna make you pay for my time."

The bad guy takes a step toward Ronald, who cautiously steps back in response. He puts the shopping cart between himself and the potential attacker.

"You think that cart's gonna help you? I'll stick it up your ass!"

The bad guy lifts the front of the cart, then slams it to the ground. The sound can be heard throughout the store.

"You're a piece of shit! You probably molest little boys."

With his left hand the bad guy sweeps out a bin of tomatoes. The green ones roll across the floor. A few ripe ones splatter. Ronald tries to de-escalate the situation.

"Look, I don't know who you are but I don't want any trouble."

"I bet you don't. You're not so tough without a deputy to protect you. Why don't we take this outside?"

Ronald is flummoxed. If the bad guy charges he'll have to run or fight back. And the thought of leading this guy on a chase through the store seems downright comical.

"The police are on their way."

Ronald turns to his right to see who spoke. The produce manager is striding toward them. Ronald turns back to see the bad guy walking slowly toward the front of the store. He looks back and says over his shoulder, "Remember, Doc. Ain't no use crying over spilled milk." Moments later he's out of sight.

"I had your back," says a woman standing next to Ronald. "One more step and I was going to throw a cantaloupe at him." The tension breaks as everyone laughs, including Ronald.

Ronald realizes the guy must have been a criminal defendant he evaluated. He has no memory of him, but the man quoted a proverb Ronald often utilized to test the ability to think abstractly.

About five minutes later a uniformed officer walks to the produce section and asks, "Who got threatened?"

Ronald meekly raises his hand.

"The store manager followed the guy to the parking lot and asked us to detain him. Tell me what happened."

Ronald tells him. He adds that he probably evaluated the suspect years ago.

"Did you feel threatened?"

"Yes."

"If you identify him, we're gonna charge him with Assault. Is that what you want?"

Ronald thinks for a moment. Assault is a misdemeanor. They won't hold the guy for long.

"Yes, I guess so."

Ronald walks to the parking lot with the officer. The suspect is sitting in the back seat of a patrol vehicle. The other officer had run a warrants check and learned that the suspect is on felony probation. An arrest would be a violation. He would be taken to jail and couldn't be released until he appeared before his felony court judge.

The officer who interviewed Ronald asks, "Is that the guy?"

Ronald is uneasy, but he doesn't know what else to do.

"Yep. That's him."

The other officer steps out of the vehicle and addresses Ronald.

"Just so you know, he says he wasn't going to hurt you. He was stopping to get a sandwich when he saw you. He decided to follow you into the store and give you a piece of his mind. He said he just wanted to scare you."

"Well, mission accomplished."

The officer gives Ronald a victim information pamphlet. Included is a case number and the suspect's name, Alan Crosby. Ronald quickly finishes his shopping and drives home. At a stoplight he keeps his hands on the wheel to stop them from shaking.

Ronald unloads the groceries. He forgot the flowers. He gets the external hard drive containing digital copies of all his reports. He connects the drive to his desktop computer. He finds the report he did on Alan Crosby, who was charged with Grand Theft and Dealing in Stolen Property in 2013. When Ronald evaluated him, Crosby presented as if he could not answer even simple questions regarding his charges or the court process. He later provided detailed information regarding his background. Then, he made multiple errors when asked to recite the alphabet and count to ten. Ronald reported to the judge that Crosby was feigning a mental defect in an effort to be found incompetent to proceed to trial. As Ronald reviews the report, he feels confident that his evaluation was thorough and his opinion well supported. The grocery store incident was an example of a defendant lashing out in an attempt to assign responsibility for his fate to others. Crosby eventually pled guilty. He was sentenced to three years in prison followed by three years of probation.

Cody is sitting in the clubhouse lounge at 4:15. He's feeling better after his third beer. He finished with a double bogey to give him a 41 on the back nine. 79 is not a bad round, but after the strong start he was hoping for a better score. And he didn't enjoy himself. He kept thinking about how much more fun he had playing alongside Brian. Still, he reasons that everything is turning out okay. He can always find another golf partner. His debt has been wiped clean. He pocketed $5000 by betting on the Penguins and the Warriors to win the deciding games of their series. Best of all, he's going to be a father. He finishes one more beer and goes home in an Uber. The Rays are on TV tonight.

Jason sits in his recliner at 4:52. His wife should be home from work soon. He sips on a glass of pinot noir while perusing the pages of the *Failing St. Pete Times*. He searches in vain for an article untainted by liberal bias. He misses the *Tribune*. He will start dinner in a few minutes. Jason is disappointed, but not surprised, that there will be no poker tonight. He'll continue to occupy his time some other way. He can wait.

Lisa arrives home just after 5:30. She's glad there will be no game tonight. She always felt ambivalent about Ronald's devotion to poker. When they started dating, she didn't know what to make of the fact that he played poker regularly. It seemed out of character for an otherwise conventional guy who didn't smoke and rarely drank. She initially resented the idea that he would be unavailable one night a week regardless of her schedule. She accepted the arrangement by viewing it as a primitive form of male bonding. She came to see poker night as an opportunity to study or to catch up with female friends. It was certainly not an issue those years they lived apart. By the time she joined Ronald in Tampa, the Thursday night game was well established. For a year or two she did not like her house being used for an activity of no interest to her. After a while, she grew to relish the idea of having one night a week all to herself. She could maintain control of the TV remote while relaxing in pajamas in her bedroom. She accepted the game as an integral part of their life. However, in recent years she had come to view the situation as increasingly confining.

As soon as Lisa walks in the door, Ronald says, "A guy confronted me at the grocery store today. He threatened to kick my ass."

Lisa's eyes widen. "What? Who was it?"

"Some guy I evaluated four years ago."

"What was his name?"

"Alan Crosby, if it matters. I'm fine, by the way."

"I'm sorry. Did he hurt you?"

"No. He never touched me."

"Well, what happened?"

"He surprised me in the produce section and threatened me. He left when a manager said he called the cops. They arrested him in the parking lot."

"That would have been a good time to have a gun."

Ronald is irritated. "Why? So I can shoot an unarmed man in the grocery store? Would that have been a better outcome?"

"At least we wouldn't have to worry about him anymore. Did you call that detective? This might be the guy who killed Brian and Russ."

Ronald shakes his head. "I don't think so."

"Why not?"

"It doesn't make any sense. That guy ambushed Brian and Russ in the middle of the night when they got home. No one saw him. Why would that same guy come at me in the middle of the day with a store full of witnesses? He didn't try to rob me or hurt me."

"Well, I think the detective should at least know about it and look into him. If you don't call him, I will."

Ronald sighs. "Fine, I'll call him tomorrow. Let's eat something."

After tonight, that call will not be necessary.

It is just after 8:30 when a patrol vehicle passes in front of Cody King's house. A moment later it's out of sight. Lucas parks his Jeep a block from the residence. Tonight, he is going to rob and possibly kill Cody. He intended to follow him home from the poker game. That plan had worked well with Brian Ridge and Russ Nichols, although he failed to anticipate that Russ might not be carrying any money. Regardless, Lucas had learned there would be no poker game tonight. He decided to go with an alternative plan. He knew where Cody lived and knew that he had a lot of money. The surest way to get paid was through a home invasion. Lucas had experience with that.

Life has been difficult for Lucas. He never knew his father. During his formative years he lived in Tampa with his drug-addicted mother. He was placed in foster care at age six due to neglect. He lived in several foster homes. He was physically abused in two of them. None of his foster parents elected to adopt him. By the time he was a teenager his frequent transgressions included truancy, fighting and theft. He began using and selling drugs. His first juvenile arrest occurred when he was fourteen. While in a detention facility an adversary cut the left side of his face with a contraband razor. A sloppy job of suturing left him with a prominent scar. He was expelled from public school and attended high school at an alternative school. At seventeen he dropped out of the tenth grade. He ran away from his foster home and began life on his own. He held a series of unskilled labor jobs, but none for more than two months. Over the next four years he was arrested six times for charges including Possession of Cocaine, Battery, Grand Theft and Burglary. He failed to complete probation several times. He served a brief prison sentence in 1996. The next year he was charged with Armed Burglary, Robbery with a Firearm and Possession of a Firearm by a Convicted Felon following a home invasion. He was convicted and sentenced to twenty years in prison. Florida law required that he serve at least 85% of the sentence, meaning he could not be released for seventeen years.

While awaiting trial, Lucas learned that his girlfriend Melanie was pregnant. She gave birth to a daughter later that year. Melanie refused to allow Lucas to see the girl until he could show he was rehabilitated. He had always justified his rule-breaking by rationalizing that the world had not dealt him a fair hand. For the first time he felt motivated to rectify his behavior. While in prison he availed himself of all the programs the Department of Corrections had to offer. He earned a high school diploma. He completed a substance use education program. He learned carpentry and welding in vocational programs. He took pains to avoid disciplinary violations that would delay his release. Melanie did not allow their daughter to visit him, but she eventually permitted letters and phone calls. Lucas completed the sentence and returned to the Tampa area in 2014. He was determined to be worthy of being the father of Sabrina Ward.

A former cellmate invited Lucas to share a mobile home in Gibsonton, a rural community southeast of Tampa. Lucas took a construction job. He attended weekly AA meetings and abstained from alcohol and drugs. After he saved a little money and bought an old Jeep, he contacted Melanie about seeing Sabrina. Melanie was married for the third time and had two younger children. She and her husband were at wits' end when it came to Sabrina. She had dropped out of school and was not working. She spent most nights at parties where she indulged her penchants for substance use and promiscuity. Melanie and her husband were happy to give Lucas a chance to redirect Sabrina. For the next year he spent as much time as he could with her. He expressed regret for his absence and tried to convince her to avoid the path he had taken. They began to develop a rapport, but her behavior did not change. In 2015 she was murdered while walking home from a party late at night.

The foundation of the new life Lucas was building suddenly crumbled. He resumed drinking whiskey and smoking crack. Over the next two years he lost several jobs. He and his roommate were evicted from the mobile home. He usually stayed in homeless shelters or in his Jeep. The only work he could find was through labor pools. He attended court proceedings in the criminal case against Sabrina's killer. He resolved that no outcome other than a death sentence would be acceptable. He cared little about anything or anyone else.

Lucas dons mask and gloves and steps out of the Jeep. He tucks the gun into his waistband. The sound of distant thunder getting louder tells him a storm is approaching. That's okay. He plans to be quick. He leaves the engine running so he won't have to worry about whether the vehicle will start again. He walks past four houses and slips to the east side of Cody's residence. He climbs a fence and lands softly on the grass. He makes his way to an unlit area of the deck. He creeps to the edge of a sliding glass door and peeks into the interior. A breakfast nook and adjacent kitchen are dark and unoccupied. Beyond that is an illumi-nated room. Lucas can hear a television set blaring crowd noise from what sounds like a Rays game. He doesn't see anyone. He can approach the room unseen.

The storm is getting closer. When Lucas sees lightning flash, he forces open the sliding door, simultaneous with the clap of thunder. He listens for a security alarm, but none sounds. He steps into the breakfast nook and draws the gun. As he approaches, he hears the low growl of a dog. Lucas bursts into the room and points the gun at Cody, who is sitting alone on one side of an L-shaped sofa. In an instant, Radley the German shepherd springs from the other side of the sofa. He lunges at Lucas. Lucas fires a shot, which misses Radley and punctures the sofa. The dog continues to charge. Lucas turns and raises his left arm in a defensive maneuver. Radley sinks his teeth into the intruder's forearm and drags him to the floor. As they struggle, Cody runs out of the room and yells to Cindy, "Lock your door and call 9-1-1!"

Lucas strikes Radley with the gun, but the dog maintains his grip. Lucas pulls the trigger. Radley is struck in the left flank. He releases and yelps. Blood spurts all over Lucas. The impact of the blast sends Radley rolling across the floor. Lucas doesn't wait to see if the dog recovers. He knows it's time to abort. He scrambles to his feet and runs out the way he came, leaving a trail of blood droplets in his wake. It's raining now and he quickly gets soaked. He circles back to the east side of the house, hops the fence and sprints for the Jeep. As he slides into the driver's seat, he pauses to remove his shirt and wrap it around his bleeding forearm. He hears sirens in the distance. He stashes the mask and gloves in the console, puts the vehicle in gear and drives out of the area at the speed limit. Twenty minutes later he pulls into the parking lot of the Seminole Heights motel that has been his home for almost two weeks.

Lucas enters a ground floor room and goes straight to the bathroom. He looks for rubbing alcohol, but he has none. He grabs a partially full pint bottle of whiskey, takes a swig and pours the remaining contents over the puncture wounds. He holds a washcloth over the wounds until the oozing stops. He digs through his duffel bag and finds a pair of scissors. A few snips later the ponytail is gone. He strips off his clothes, takes a shower and puts on clean clothes. He bundles the wet clothes, the soiled washcloth and the disembodied ponytail and walks to a dumpster. He disposes of the bundle and returns to the room. After trimming more hair, he sits and contemplates the immediate future. He has already made plans to start work on an oil platform off the coast of Alaska. On June 23rd he will sell the Jeep and take a bus to Atlanta. From there he will fly to Anchorage. After tonight's debacle he knows he needs to leave town sooner than later. But first, he has one more poker player to kill.

The Fourth Thursday

ANDY BARLOW spreads three case files across the top of his desk. It is 8:45 on the morning of June 22nd. A week has passed since the home invasion at Cody King's residence. The ballistics report confirmed that the 9-millimeter slug embedded in Cody's sofa was from the same gun used to kill Brian Ridge and Russ Nichols. The bullet removed from Radley the German shepherd during surgery was also a match. There had been no activity on the credit cards taken from the two murder victims. Witnesses from the last two incidents reported seeing a white male leave the scene in a red, older model Jeep Cherokee after shots were fired. This was confirmed by security cameras. The license tag was not visible. Cody described a white male in his thirties or forties, six feet tall, thin, with a ponytail and multiple tattoos. Andy is awaiting DNA results from blood samples collected at Cody's house.

Andy looks over the files again, hoping to see what he's missing. The incidents were clearly connected to the poker game, but how? Either the assailant is familiar with the game or has a connection to somebody who is. How were the victims chosen? The motive seemed to be robbery. Brian's wallet was emptied of cash and credit cards. Russ Nichols' wallet was taken. Why did the assailant kill Brian and Russ? Would he have killed Cody had it not been for the dog? Why hasn't he used the credit cards?

After Brian was killed, Andy considered the possibility that Cody might have paid someone to do it. None of the other players liked Brian, but only Cody had an obvious reason to kill him. He owed Brian $100,000, which he probably didn't want to repay. Paying for a murder would not be out of character for a man driven to desperation by gambling debts and substance use. Cody did have a criminal record, but nothing involving violence. And why would he have Russ killed? It also seemed unlikely that Cody would stage a home invasion involving gunfire and the wounding of his dog. Such elaborate schemes only happen in books and movies.

Andy turns his attention to the other players, none of whom has a criminal record. All are educated professionals who appear to be financially comfortable. Four are lawyers. Andy smiles as he asks himself whether being a lawyer makes one more or less likely to commit murder. The group seems to be divided into two cliques. Ronald, Scott, David, Matt, Dick and Robert had played together for fifteen years or more. Brian, Russ, Cody and the others joined the game more recently. All of the newer players live in South Tampa. Brian, Russ and Cody were assaulted at their South Tampa residences. Was that because the perpetrator lives in South Tampa? If so, he was more likely to be acquainted with a player from South Tampa than one of the others. Who among them other than Cody had a plausible reason to kill Brian or Russ? Rick Williams insisted he was joking when he asked if he had to kill somebody to move up on the list. Neither was there any reason to suggest Bruce Silver or Bill Mumphrey were involved.

That leaves the longtime players to consider. Maybe one of them resented the newcomers. All of them seemed to dislike Brian. He had hustled them out of a lot of money, and they knew it. But the attacks on Russ and Cody were a couple of puzzle pieces that didn't fit. It sounded as though they were both net losers in the game. There had to be another reason. Andy carefully considers whether Scott, David, Matt, Dick or Robert had any conceivable reason to plot against the three victims. All are family men who work full-time. During their interviews, none of them acted as if they were hiding anything.

What about Ronald and Jason? Both are retired, so they would have more time on their hands to plan something like this. In Ronald's case, it seemed strange for a man barely sixty to stay home while his wife was still working. Was it a coincidence that the murders happened so soon after his retirement? Neither Jason nor Ronald has children. Does that speak to a defect in their ability to form emotional attachments? Both acted as if being interviewed was an imposition. During his first interview, Ronald seemed cold and logical in response to Brian's death. But if he got rid of Brian for winning too much, why would he try to have two consistent losers bumped off? As for Jason, he made clear that Brian's presence was the main reason he dropped out of the game. Then he refused a second interview. Would he have Brian, Russ and Cody killed just to get back into the game? Andy decides to ask both to return for another interview.

Ronald is finishing breakfast when his flip phone rings. It's Jason. Ronald warily answers. Surely Jason's not still lobbying to resume the game.

"Hello."

"Ronald! That detective called me again!"

"What did he want?"

"He asked me to come for another interview. I told him to drop dead. I have nothing more to say."

"Your call."

"How long until you think we can play again? I don't have that much time left, you know."

"Not sure. The detective already told us to take a break for a while. After last week I'm sure he hasn't changed his mind."

Ronald sees that he has an incoming call. It's Detective Barlow. He decides to let it go to voicemail as Jason keeps talking.

"Hopefully this guy will be caught soon. How about lunch and then to the Hard Rock to play 5-10? I've been itching to get back at it."

Ronald thinks for a moment. Why not? "Where will you be?"

"I'm at party headquarters but I leave at 11. You can pick me up at home at 11:30."

Ronald hangs up and listens to the voicemail. Detective Barlow wants to talk to him again. Ronald doesn't feel like dealing with it today. He'll call him back tomorrow or Monday.

Jason is waiting outside his home when Ronald arrives. He eases into the front passenger seat.

"Hi, Jason. Where are we eating?"

"Up to you, sir. I am an omnivore."

They settle on Acropolis in New Tampa. They talk while munching on their Greek salads.

"So it was the same guy who attacked all three?"

"Sounds like it," responds Ronald. "The detective said it was the same gun and witnesses from Russ and Cody's neighborhoods saw the same vehicle."

"What kind of vehicle?"

"He wouldn't say, which kind of irritated me. I know it's important to hold back some information. But I'd like to know what to look for in case I'm next."

"I would think so. Did he say what kind of gun?"

"No. He did say he sent some samples for DNA. Cody said there was blood all over the place."

Jason's bushy eyebrows raise. "Really? So if the guy's got a record they'll be able to pin him down."

"I certainly hope so. I want my life back."

Jason doesn't voice what he's thinking: *so would Brian and Russ.*

"And it wasn't the guy from the grocery store?"

"Couldn't have been. The detective confirmed that guy was still in jail. It wasn't him at Cody's house."

"So you think that was just a coincidence?"

Ronald shrugs. "I don't know what to think." He adds in the tip and signs his receipt. "Let's go play poker."

Andy breaks for lunch at 12:15. When he returns, there is an envelope from the Florida Department of Law Enforcement on his desk. He opens it and sees the results of DNA testing on the blood samples taken from Cody King's residence. Most reveal canine DNA. Two of them are a match for Lucas Ward. Andy sits at his computer and goes to work. He reviews the suspect's criminal record and notes that he was released from prison in 2014. A few months later he purchased a red 2001 Jeep Cherokee. He is still listed as the registered owner. Andy calls Lee Turner and asks him to bring Cody to the station to look at a photographic line-up.

Ronald and Jason get to the Hard Rock poker room at 12:50. They join the list for a new 5-10 game, which will start at 1:00. The game will be nine-handed. Jason slides into seat number 6. Ronald chooses seat 7. He would prefer seat 5 at the center of the table, but Ronald doesn't want Jason to have position on him all afternoon. Jason buys $2000 worth of chips. Ronald buys in for $1000. He has another $1000 in his pocket.

Cash games in poker rooms are slightly different from home games. The house supplies the dealers, who rotate in thirty-minute shifts. Before each hand the dealer makes sure the button and the blinds are positioned correctly. He shuffles and deals the cards but does not deal himself a hand. He manages the pot and resolves any disputes. A small percentage of each pot is retained for the house. Dealers earn most of their money from tips, so it is customary to tip after winning a hand.

Ronald plays the first two orbits like a boxer keeping his distance while probing for weakness. He is dealt mostly garbage hands and folds all of them before the flop. He tries to get a feel for each player. Meanwhile, Jason wins a nice pot with a Jack high flush after the guy in seat 2 bets into him on the turn and the river with two pair.

Ronald surmises that the guys in seat 5 and seat 8 are good, aggressive players. He knows Jason is as well. The others seem sound, with two exceptions. The guy in seat 2 is a quiet, older, Asian man who keeps putting an unlit cigarette in his mouth. By 1:20 he is on his second beer. The guy in seat 9 is young and loquacious. He wears a T-shirt that reads "Shit Happens–Don't Step In It." Both play loose and recklessly at times. They see almost every flop and tend to overplay their hands. Some good players would loosen up and try to play lots of hands against them. The rationale is that reckless players will make more mistakes and can be outplayed in the long run. There are downsides to this strategy. If you play a lot of hands, you need to win some of them by bluffing. Reckless players tend to be "sticky," meaning it's difficult to get them to fold. And if you play a lot of hands against reckless players and they get lucky, you can find yourself down several thousand dollars while hoping the tide turns.

Ronald is more comfortable with an approach that better suits his style of play. Because reckless players tend to play hands to the river, Ronald has found that the best way to extract money from them is to "show them a hand." You want to play big pots against them when you have the best hand. This strategy requires patience. You must fold poor and marginal starting hands, playing only pairs, big cards and suited connectors. There is a downside to this strategy as well. If your play is too tight, other players will notice. Even reckless players might fold when you enter a pot because they know you are playing only premium hands.

For the first two hours Ronald folds almost every hand without seeing the flop. He sees two hands good enough to raise to $40 pre-flop. The first is AQ. The other is KK. Both times everyone folds to his raise, even the guys in seat 2 and seat 9. He sticks to his strategy of playing tight. Jason takes notice.

"Ronald, if you're just here to watch, why don't you go stand on the rail?"

Spectators stand behind a rail. The guys in seats 8 and 9 hear the comment and chuckle. Ronald starts to admonish Jason for pointing this out, but he stops himself. He knows the other players can see how tight he's playing. He decides to mix it up a little more. He tries to limp into the next pot with 98 off-suit, but folds when the guy in seat 9 raises. His chip stack is less than $600. He buys another $1000 worth of chips.

Ronald's first big chance comes at 3:18. Seat 2 is on the button. Seats 3 and 4 post the blinds. Seat 5 limps for $10. Jason folds. Ronald looks down at QJ of hearts, a hand which plays well in multi-way pots. He calls $10, as does Seat 8. Seat 9 raises to $50. Seat 1 folds. Seat 2 calls. Seats 3 and 4 fold. Seat 5 calls, as do Ronald and Seat 8. The pot is $265. Ronald has $1500 left. Five players see a flop of

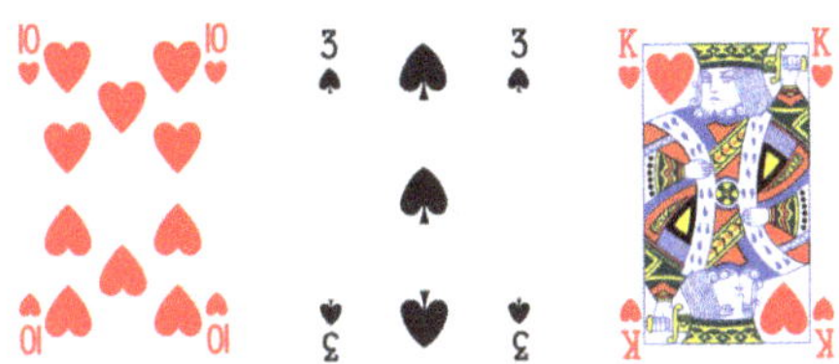

Ronald could hardly ask for a better flop. He has an open-end straight flush draw. Either the Ace of hearts or the 9 of hearts would give him a straight flush. The other seven hearts would give him the second nut flush. The other three Aces and the other three Nines would give him the nut straight. The probability of any of these cards appearing on the turn or the river is 54%.

Acting first, Seat 5 bets $250. Ronald considers his options. Folding is out of the question. He could move all in, a play known as a semi-bluff. If he is called, as many as fifteen cards would give him the winning hand on the turn or the river. He knows he would be called by any player with a set, two pair, pocket Aces or even a King with a good kicker. His odds of winning a showdown would be better than 50-50 against a pair, a little less against two pair or a set. If everyone folded, he would have to settle for a $465 profit on a potentially big hand. Better to wait and see if he can make a hand and get a big payoff. He calls the $250 bet. Seat 8 folds. Seat 9 and Seat 2 call. The pot is $1265. Ronald has $1250 remaining.

The turn card is the 7 of clubs. The board is:

That card changes nothing, other than to reduce the chances of Ronald making a hand. Seat 5 bets $600, less than half the pot. Ronald is getting good pot odds, a term which compares the likelihood of winning a hand to the potential payoff if you do. By calling he could win at least $1865 if one of his cards comes on the river. The odds are now 2:1 against him hitting his draw, but if he does the payoff would be better than 3:1. Had Seat 5 checked, Ronald would have moved all in. But Seat 5 is representing a good hand with his bet. Ronald doesn't have enough chips to pressure Seat 5 to fold. Besides, if Ronald calls it might entice one or both of the other players to call. That will make for a bigger pot if he connects on the river. He calls, diminishing his stack to $650. Seat 9 calls. Seat 2 folds. The pot is $3065.

The river card is the 3 of diamonds. The board is:

Ronald has missed everything. No flush, no straight, no nothing. Seat 5 thinks for a moment, then checks. Ronald knows he can only win the hand by betting to represent a full house or three of a kind. If he pulls it off, it would be the bluff of the year. But there are two problems. First, a bluff has to tell a convincing story. If he had a set or two pair which became a full house, he would not have slow-played the flop and the turn with both flush and straight draws possible. It is even less likely that he stayed in with a 3 and made trips on the river. The other problem is that getting both opponents to fold to a $650 bet when the pot would be over $3700 is beyond unlikely. This hand has already cost him over half his chips. No sense losing the rest. He checks, raising the white flag. Seat 9 checks. Seat 5 shows KT, giving him Kings and Tens. Seat 9 shows KQ for Kings and Threes. Ronald mucks his cards. Seat 5 takes the pot.

Cody King and Lee Turner arrive at the police station just after 3:30. Andy shows Cody five photographs of middle-aged white men with long hair. Lucas Ward's photograph is in the number four position.

"This might be hard," offers Cody. "He wore a mask, and it happened really fast."

"Take your time," says Andy. "Try to be sure before you say anything. A guess doesn't help."

Cody looks carefully at each photo, going back and forth. He finally points to number four.

"I think that's him."

"How sure are you?"

"Ninety percent."

"Good enough," says Andy. "I need you to sign here. Your lawyer can read it for you if you like."

Andy starts the process of obtaining a warrant for the arrest of Lucas Ward on charges including two counts of First Degree Murder, three counts of Armed Burglary of a Dwelling, two counts of Robbery with a Firearm and one count of Aggravated Assault with a Firearm. The warrant is approved within an hour.

Ronald hears the beep of his digital watch. It's 4:00. He has $600 left, which means he's $1400 in the hole. Jason is up over $1000. They had previously agreed to leave by 4:30 to beat the worst of the traffic. Time is running out for Ronald to turn it around.

Seat 4 is on the button. Seat 5 and Jason post the blinds. Ronald looks down at AK, usually a raising hand. But Ronald decides to play it differently. He reasons that if he raises to $40 and three or four players call, he will be out of position with a hand that probably needs help to win. If he misses the flop, which will happen two-thirds of the time, going all in would give him his best chance to win. He would have to hope everyone folds or that he pairs one of his cards on the turn or the river. He decides to limp. If anyone raises, he will move all in.

Ronald puts $10 into the pot. Seat 8 calls. Seat 9 raises to $50. Seat 1 folds. Seat 2 calls. Seat 3, Seat 4, Seat 5 and Jason fold. Ronald is okay with this development. There is $135 in the pot.

"All in," he announces. A few jaws drop. The tight player is making his stand.

Seat 8 sighs. "Too rich for me." He sends his hand to the muck.

Seat 9 quickly calls for $550. Ronald expects a heads-up showdown. But Seat 2 is contemplating the situation.

"Okay, let's gamble," he finally says. He adds $550 to the pot, making it $1825.

Both Seat 2 and Seat 9 have Ronald covered, so nobody shows their cards. After the flop either of the other two players could bet and create a side pot from which Ronald would be excluded. He can only win the main pot. The flop is:

Ronald connected with the flop. He has paired his King, giving him top pair and top kicker. Few draws are possible.

"That can't be good," says Seat 9. He smiles, as does Seat 2. They know a tight player like Ronald would not have limp-raised all in unless he had a big pair or AK. With the King on the flop, they are sure Ronald is in the lead. Both players check. The turn is a 9. The river is an 8. There is no more betting.

Ronald shows his hand. Seat 9 shows JJ. Seat 2 shows 77 and says, "Good hand." The dealer keeps $5 for the house and sends $1820 to Ronald. Ronald returns a $10 chip as a tip. He is suddenly less than $200 down.

"Well done, Ronald," offers Jason. "You got a hand just in time." It's almost 4:10.

A few hands later the button is on Seat 9. Seat 1 and Seat 2 post the blinds. Seat 3 limps under the gun. Seat 4 calls. Seat 5 folds. Jason calls. Ronald looks down at 55. He doesn't like to raise with small pairs, preferring to see the flop cheaply in hopes of hitting a set. He calls.

Seat 8 raises to $60. Seat 9 quickly calls. Ronald is pleased. That guy is like Cody King in a better mood. He hopes more players will enter the pot. Seat 1 folds but Seat 2 calls, as usual. Seat 3 folds. Seat 4 calls. Jason folds and says, "All yours, Ronald." Ronald calls, closing the action.

Five players will see the flop. The pot is $325. The flop is:

Ronald has flopped middle set. He trails only 77 (top set) and 64, which would be a straight. It is highly unlikely that even a reckless player called $60 pre-flop with 64. He hopes somebody will bet and build the pot. He is disappointed when Seat 2 and Seat 4 check in turn.

Ronald could bet, but he's certain Seat 8 will bet with what is probably a big pair. He might even make a continuation bet with AK. Ronald would then have a chance to check-raise. He checks. Seat 8 bets $250. Perfect, thinks Ronald. Then perfect gets better. Seat 9 raises to $700. Seat 2 and Seat 4 fold. It's back to Ronald. He has $1735 left. Time to put the hammer down.

"All in."

Seat 8 looks deflated. He stares at Ronald and thinks out loud. "Thought I had the best hand, but I guess I'm beat." His cards find the muck.

It is $1040 to Seat 9. He flashes a wide grin.

"What the Hell. I call." He pushes the chips to the center. The pot is $4045, minus $5 for the house.

Ronald shows his set. Seat 9 winces and shows 76, giving him top pair and a gut shot straight draw. He needs a 4 for a straight or, even less likely, running (consecutive) cards to make a full house.

The turn is a Deuce. The river is a Ten. Seat 8 slaps the top of the table with both hands.

"Damn! I threw away pocket Tens." His set of Tens would have won. The dealer pushes $4040 Ronald's way. Ronald sends back $25 as a tip. In two hands he has gone from $1400 down to over $2000 ahead.

It is 4:21. Jason and Ronald stay for three more hands, after which Jason would have to post the big blind. Ronald folds two garbage hands pre-flop. On the last hand Jason limps from under the gun. Ronald looks down at AJ. An hour ago, he would have called or raised with this hand. But he folds. Even if he pairs the Ace, he would still be behind AK and AQ. He does not want to get involved in a pot large enough to carve out a chunk of his winnings. He stands and begins putting his chips into a rack, a signal that he's done. He and other players exchange cordial goodbyes.

The flop is:

Ronald is pleased to see he would have missed the flop. No reason to second-guess. Jason folds to the first bet. Ronald walks to the cage to cash in his chips. Jason is a minute behind him. The drive home will be pleasant.

Cody gets home at 4:42. Radley greets him affectionately. The dog's wound is healing well. Cody opens the refrigerator and takes out a bottle of Samuel Adams. He helps Radley onto the sofa and sits next to him. He strokes the dog's head while sipping his beer. When he joined the Thursday night poker game, he didn't sign up for robbery and murder. After today, the ugliness should soon be over.

Ronald pulls in front of Jason's townhome at 5:05. Before exiting, Jason asks, "Do you think there's any need to worry tonight?"

"Worry about what?"

"About the guy who's killing your poker players! He seems to work one day a week, and today's the day."

"Maybe he's French."

Jason laughs heartily before responding.

"Are you taking any precautions?"

"I guess. Precautions are built into my routine. But I'm not too worried. The guy seems to operate out of South Tampa. With no poker game, and after what happened with Cody, he's probably moved on."

"I hope you're right. I hope to see you soon."

Jason steps out of the car and watches as Ronald drives out of sight. He opens the front door and removes his shoes in the foyer. He pours a glass of cabernet sauvignon. Before he sits, he decides to check his guns. He removes two 9-millimeter pistols from the gun cabinet, a Glock and a Walther. He leaves the Taurus where it is. He verifies that the Glock and the Walther are loaded. Whatever happens, he'll be ready.

Andy Barlow leaves the station at 5:13 to serve the warrant on Lucas Ward at his last known address. He rides in a marked vehicle with Pete, a uniformed officer. Andy hopes Lucas will surrender peacefully. He wants to question Lucas to determine whether he acted alone. Because the residence is located in unincorporated Hillsborough County, two sheriff's deputies will meet them to assist as needed.

Ronald walks in the door at 5:21. He looks forward to Lisa getting home from work so he can tell her about his day. He feels even better after he logs on to the bank account he used for his practice. A $2600 deposit was posted today, the payment for testimony in his final case. He has no other payments pending. It finally seems like he's fully retired, and it feels good.

Ronald's final case was as grisly as it was heartbreaking. He was retained by the Office of the Public Defender to evaluate Richard Crump, a thirty-four-year-old man diagnosed with schizophrenia at age nineteen. Crump had been hospitalized in psychiatric facilities dozens of times, but rarely for more than a few days. He had been arrested almost as often, usually on minor charges. While hospitalized or incarcerated his condition would improve once he resumed taking antipsychotic medication. When he returned to the community, he was usually placed in supervised housing and scheduled for outpatient appointments to receive his medication. Within a few weeks he would invariably leave his housing facility, stop taking the medication and decompensate. During psychotic episodes he heard voices and had delusional beliefs about people being possessed by demons. One night in 2015 he experienced a severe episode. The voices told him he needed to kill a virgin to drive out the devil and save Mankind. He took a kitchen knife from his cousin's apartment and set out to do just that.

Shortly after 2 a.m. Crump encountered Sabrina Ward as she was walking home from a party. She was seventeen years old. At the party she drank vodka and took ecstasy. She had more than one sexual partner. Nevertheless, the voices told Crump that Sabrina was the virgin he was seeking. He stabbed her thirty-seven times. When police detained him an hour later, he was carrying the knife and was covered in blood. He told the officers everything was okay because he had killed the devil.

Ronald evaluated Crump later that week. He concluded that Crump was in the throes of a psychotic episode when he stabbed Sabrina. The case went to trial in April 2017. Ronald testified that Crump was legally insane at the time of the stabbing. His testimony was contentious, dramatic and ultimately compelling. A few days later the jury decided that Crump was not guilty by reason of insanity. The judge committed him to a state psychiatric facility.

Ronald did not notice that Lucas Ward was in the courtroom during his testimony. Lucas had come to court every day to see that his daughter's killer got justice. During pre-trial hearings he listened intently as the attorneys argued about what evidence could be introduced. He heard gruesome details from the autopsy report. He seethed when the defense attorney wanted to introduce Sabrina's substance use and promiscuity, as if that had anything to do with why she was killed. During the trial, Lucas was especially galled by Ronald's testimony. Ronald painted the murdering monster as a tragic figure in need of treatment, not punishment. He showed no sympathy for Sabrina or her family. He never even mentioned her name, referring to her as "the alleged victim." During a recess Lucas told Melanie "If that animal gets away with murder, I'm gonna f---ing kill that shrink and that P.D."

Lisa gets home at 5:38. Ronald hugs and kisses her before she puts her purse on the counter.

"Hi, Honey. How was your day?"

"It was a day. The guy with sepsis took a turn for the worse. I'm worried about him."

Ronald isn't really listening.

"I'd say my day was better."

Lisa tries to mask her annoyance.

"Okay. Tell me about your day."

"I had lunch with Jason, then we went to the Hard Rock. I hardly won a hand for three hours and was down $1400. Then, in fifteen minutes I won two huge pots and wound up ahead $2000."

Lisa feigns interest. "Wow! That's great. Did you have fun?"

"Yes. Jason and I had a good day."

"Must be nice."

"Then, I get home and check my business account. I got paid for the Richard Crump case, my last testimony. That's it. I'm done. I can close that account tomorrow. So now we have $4600 more than we had this morning. And all I did was eat lunch and play poker."

Lisa forces a smile. Ronald senses that he has overwhelmed her before she had a chance to decompress.

"I'm sorry I cut you off. Tell me about the guy with sepsis."

"No, that's okay. There isn't much more to tell. Why don't we eat something and you can tell me more about poker."

"Do you want to pour yourself a glass of wine?"

"No. I don't feel like drinking tonight."

It is after 6:30 when Andy Barlow and Officer Pete meet the deputies about a mile from the target residence, a mobile home in Gibsonton. After formulating a plan, they make the short trip in separate vehicles. They park on the road. The deputies unholster their firearms and walk on opposite sides of the domicile, covering any doors and windows that could be used as escape routes. Andy and Officer Pete walk to the front door. The interior is lit and they can hear muffled voices. There is no doorbell. Andy taps on the door. He waits fifteen seconds and taps again.

A young man opens the door. He has dark hair and a dark complexion. Andy towers over him. He shows the man his badge and tells him they're here to see Lucas Ward.

"No hablo inglés."

Andy shows the man a photograph of Lucas. "Is he here?"

The man looks at the photograph. *"No, no está aquí. Él no vive aquí."*

Andy knows just enough Spanish to comprehend. Lucas doesn't live here. He sends Officer Pete to trade places with one of the deputies, a Spanish speaker. The deputy arrives within a minute.

"Ask him if we can come inside and take a look." The deputy translates.

"*Sí, Sí. ¡Pasen!*"

Andy and the deputy walk through the doorway. The interior is small, but clean and well maintained. A young woman in the kitchen is washing dishes. Two school-age children kneel at a coffee table, doing homework. A toddler is playing with blocks.

"Ask him if we can look around to make sure he's not here."

The man readily agrees. *He has nothing to hide,* thinks Andy. They won't find Lucas here. But they made the trip and they have to cover all the bases. Beyond the living area are two small bedrooms, two closets and a bathroom. No place to hide. The search takes less than five minutes. Andy questions the man and his wife as the deputy translates. They have been renting the place for about a year. They don't know who lived there before them. Their landlady is an elderly woman named Mrs. Corbett. She lives in Sun City Center, a retirement community ten miles farther south. The woman gives Andy the phone number. Andy apologizes for the intrusion and thanks them for their help.

The four lawmen walk to their vehicles. Andy thanks the deputies and releases them back to their regular duties. He has to call Mrs. Corbett. Until then, he has no idea where the search will lead. Officer Pete starts the vehicle and runs the air conditioner. At 7:14 it's still 88 degrees. They might as well be comfortable while Andy makes the call. He dials the number.

"Hello."

"Mrs. Corbett?"

"Yes. Who is this?"

"I'm Detective Barlow with the Tampa Police Department. I'm here at your rental home in Gibsonton. I'm trying to find somebody who used to live here."

"Is it those Mexicans? Did they clear out? I knew I shouldn't have rented to Mexicans!"

"No ma'am. It's not..."

"My son Bob said it would be okay. Juan works for Bob. Bob said he's a good worker and has a nice family. He said they needed a place to stay they could afford. But I knew something like this would happen. Was it Juan? What did he do? Was it drugs?"

"No ma'am. We just searched the place and there are no drugs there."

"Then why are you looking for him? Why did they leave?"

"Ma'am, they didn't leave. They're still here and everything's fine. We're not looking for Juan. We're looking for Lucas Ward."

"Oh, him. That's the guy who used to live there with my nephew Erik. Erik, he's a piece of work. Do you know what he did?"

"No ma'am, but…"

"He needed a place to stay so I said he could stay at my place in Gibsonton. It was vacant. I let him stay there for $400 a month plus utilities. Try finding a place for 400 a month. Then I find out he's letting Lucas stay there. And guess what?"

"What?"

"Lucas was paying Erik 200 a month. I never saw any of it. I said wait a minute. I didn't say two ex-cons could stay there. We eventually worked it out. I said they could both stay if they paid 600 a month. It was okay for about a year. Then they stopped paying. Three months, not a cent. So Bob paid them a visit. They weren't working, just sitting around, drinking and using drugs. And the place was a wreck. So I told them to get out."

"When did they leave?"

"Lucas left right away. Erik stayed two or three more months. Finally, Bob told him if he didn't leave we were calling the cops. Erik wanted no part of the cops. He left the next day. We cleaned up the place and rented it to the Mexicans before Erik could change his mind and try to come back. Believe it or not, I've been better off renting to the Mexicans. They pay 800 a month, and they pay on time. Plus, they keep the place clean."

"Let's get back to Lucas. When did he leave?"

"Sometime last spring. March or April."

"Have you been in contact with him since then?"

"No. No reason to. I can't get any more money from him. He didn't sign a lease or anything."

"Do you have his telephone number?"

"No, but Erik might."

Andy senses an opportunity to exit.

"Will you give me Erik's number, please?"

"Sure, if you want it. I need to look it up. Good luck with that. That kid's a loser, always has been. You can't believe a word he says. He went back to jail, but he got out. Here's the number."

Andy writes down the number.

"Mrs. Corbett, I've gotta go now but it has been a delight. Thank you for all your help. Goodbye, ma'am."

"Goodbye."

Andy ends the call and sighs. It is 7:26. He looks at Officer Pete. "It could be a long night. Let's go get some coffee."

They get a caffeine boost at a McDonald's drive-thru. Officer Pete pulls into a parking spot and keeps the engine running. They still have three-quarters of a tank of fuel. After a few sips Andy is ready to make the next call. He's determined not to waste time. Erik answers on the third ring.

"Hello."

"Erik, this is Detective Barlow with the Tampa Police Department. I'm looking for Lucas Ward. I hope you can help me find him."

"Why? What did he do?"

"We're investigating some pretty serious charges and we need to talk to him as soon as possible. Can you tell me where he's living now?"

"I just got on probation for a cocaine charge and I'm trying to stay out of trouble. Whatever he did I ain't had nothing to do with."

"Erik, I don't have any reason to think you did. I just need your help finding him. His last known address he was rooming with you in Gibsonton, but you guys aren't there anymore. Did you two stay in touch?"

"For a little bit, but I haven't talked to him since last year. I don't know where he's living now. And I lost my phone and all my contacts, so I don't even have his number."

"Do you know somebody who might know where he is?"

"Maybe, but I'd rather not get mixed up in this. Like I said, I'm trying to steer clear of trouble."

"Who do you know who might know where he is?"

"The guy who used to sell us crack."

"Do you have his number?"

"Yeah, but I don't want to get him involved. I shouldn't even be talking to him. That could get me violated."

"I understand that, Erik. You don't have to tell me his name or tell him what this is about. Look at it this way. If you help me with this, that's something I can tell your probation officer. And when it comes time to decide whether you've done enough to terminate probation, you'll have some extra credit. It tells the judge you'd rather be with the good guys than the bad guys."

Erik pauses. "What do I say?"

"Just tell him you're trying to find Lucas and does he know where he is. That should be enough. If he wants to know why, tell him you've got something that belongs to Lucas and you want to give it to him."

"Yeah, that should be good. When do you want me to call him?"

"Right now. Call me back at this number and tell me what you find out."

Andy hangs up and waits. He's almost done with his coffee when his phone rings. It's Erik.

"Hello. What did you find out?"

"Last week the guy took crack to Lucas at the Shangri-La Motel on Nebraska Avenue in Seminole Heights. I got you his phone number, too."

"Thanks, Erik. I'll tell your probation officer you've been a big help."

Andy records the information. He won't need the phone number unless they don't find Lucas at the motel. It is 7:55.

Ronald hasn't moved from his recliner since dinner. He keeps flipping channels. There isn't much to watch. Just after 8 he settles on a College

World Series game. Watchable, but he'd rather be playing poker. He misses the guys. Lisa goes to the bedroom.

Andy and Officer Pete arrive at the motel. It's after 8:30 and getting dark. Among the vehicles scattered in the parking lot is an old Jeep Cherokee. The exterior looks to be a dingy white. Andy tells Officer Pete to run the plate. Within a minute he says, "It's not a match. Could he have painted it and switched the plate?"

Andy shakes his head. The paint doesn't look new.

They find the office. Andy rings the bell. A desk clerk quickly responds. Andy flashes his badge.

"Can you tell me if Lucas Ward is staying here?"

The clerk checks the register and finds no one by that name. Andy shows him a photograph of Lucas.

"Have you seen this guy?"

The clerk looks closely.

"Yeah. That's the guy staying in room 23." He looks back at the register. "He checked in on June 2nd under the name Will Lucas. He paid cash for a week in advance. He paid for another week on the 9th and again on the 16th. He's supposed to check out tomorrow morning unless he pays to extend again. What's this about?"

"We have a warrant for his arrest. I need you to get a key and take us to his room."

The three men walk down the corridor that faces Nebraska Avenue. They turn left at the corner and stop at the third room. The curtains are drawn, and the room is dark.

"Wait behind us," Andy tells the clerk. Andy knocks on the door. There is no response. Andy waits twenty seconds and knocks again. No response. He asks the clerk, "Where's the light switch?"

"Inside the door to the left."

"Open the door and step back. If anybody shoots run back to your office and call 9-1-1."

Andy and Officer Pete draw their guns. The clerk opens the door and steps behind them. Andy flips the light switch and they burst into the lighted room. The time is 8:48.

At 8:49 Lucas Ward pulls up to the keypad for the entrance gate to Ronald Turner's neighborhood. He enters the digits 2 9 3 1 followed by the * sign. The gate slowly opens. Lucas finds an area away from a streetlight and parks his red Jeep. He leaves the engine running. He confirms that his gun is loaded. He puts on the mask and gloves. He contemplates the task ahead. Brian Ridge is dead because he turned around. Russ Nichols died because he resisted. But Lucas is going to kill Ronald Turner for Sabrina. The dashboard clock reads 8:58. Two minutes later his cell phone rings.

At 9:00 Ronald steps into the garage after disarming the security system. He's carrying a full trash bag from the kitchen. He opens the large, green bin and deposits the bag. He then opens the garage door and begins rolling the bin to the curb. On most such nights Ronald would stop to gaze at the sky for a view of the moon and other celestial objects. Tonight, he knows the moon will not rise for several hours. The cloud cover prevents him from seeing much in the way of planets or stars. He arrives at the curb and pauses briefly to look at the sky. As he turns to walk back to the garage, he sees a masked man on the sidewalk in front of the house next door. He's walking briskly in Ronald's direction. He then breaks into a dead run. Ronald freezes long enough to see that the man is carrying a gun. Ronald bolts for the garage. A plan instantly flashes across his mind. He needs to get into the house, lock the door, call 9-1-1 and find his gun.

Lucas begins shooting as soon as Ronald starts running. He doesn't want Ronald to make it into the garage. Lucas fires several shots in rapid succession. Most of them miss and ricochet off the driveway or garage walls. One of them hits the tailgate of the Audi. The fourth or fifth shot strikes Ronald below the left hip, shattering the femur. Ronald screams and tumbles face down onto the driveway. He tries to crawl the last few feet into the garage. Lucas, now on the driveway, slows to a walk. He is determined to savor the moment. He overtakes Ronald at the edge of the garage, aims for the base of the skull and fires. The bullet enters the back of the neck just right of the midline. Ronald emits a gurgling sound, but he's still moving. Lucas aims and pulls the trigger again. Click. Empty.

Lisa steps out of the dark garage and faces Lucas. She points the Ruger and fires a shot that strikes the left side of his chest. He drops his gun and falls to his knees. She advances two steps and fires again, this time striking Lucas below the left eye. He falls to the left. His body jerks but he does not move again.

Lisa discards the Ruger and turns her attention to Ronald. He is groaning and trying to move. She shouts for help at the top of her lungs. She kneels and uses her robe to apply pressure to the wounds. When a neighbor approaches, she yells, "Call 9-1-1!" She instructs a second neighbor to use his shirt to put pressure on the hip wound while she presses on Ronald's neck. Other neighbors arrive and gasp in horror. Some gather around Lucas. One of them says, "This guy's gone." Lisa shrieks, "Don't touch him! Don't touch the guns!" The neighbors are startled by her fury as they stand back to wait for first responders. Lisa can hear the sirens. She bends to look at Ronald's face and says, "Hold on, Honey." In that instant she watches the life drain from his eyes.

The Fifth Thursday

I T IS 8:37 ON THE MORNING of June 29th. Andy Barlow sits at his desk to review his report pertaining to the three murders as well as the home invasion involving Cody King. Andy completed the report last night, but he wanted to sleep on it before submitting it. He peruses the document page by page, looking for any reason to extend the investigation. From the evidence it is clear that Lucas Ward committed all of the offenses. Ballistics confirmed that the gun recovered from the Turners' driveway was the one used in the shootings. It was reported stolen two years ago. The autopsy report revealed that Lucas had healing wounds on the left forearm consistent with a dog bite. He had not used the credit cards he took from Brian Ridge and Russ Nichols. The cards were not among his belongings at the motel. Those belongings included about $6000 in cash, less than what he was estimated to have taken from Brian. A key witness reported that Lucas uttered a threat against Ronald and the public defender in court. Sabrina's mother Melanie confirmed this, but she thought he was just blowing off steam. Andy's theory is that Lucas intended to murder Ronald because of his role in the trial of Sabrina's killer. His attempts to rob the others were designed to obscure his primary objective. There was no evidence that he was paid to commit the murders. If anyone else was involved, it was someone who fed information to Lucas about Ronald and the poker game.

Andy had contacted the homeowners' association to determine how Lucas got past the gate. He used a code registered to a couple who moved out of the neighborhood a few weeks earlier. Andy interviewed the couple over the phone. They denied knowing Lucas and had no idea how he got their code, which was their house number. They volunteered that they had freely shared the code with family members, friends, lawn men, pool men, delivery drivers and anyone else who needed it. They said they had never been too concerned about security because they believed it was a safe neighborhood. They sent Andy a list of people who knew the code. Andy interviewed most of them. None had any known ties to Lucas.

Cell phone records revealed that Lucas made or received calls from only three numbers in the thirty days before his death. He made four calls to the man identified as the drug dealer. Andy interviewed the dealer and cleared him of involvement in the murders. Lucas received nine calls from a number registered to an anonymous phone. Four of those calls were placed from a public park in Pasco County. The others appeared to be from a northbound vehicle on I-275 near downtown Tampa. Andy had interviewed Lisa, the poker players, the neighbors, the housekeeper, the pool man and the lawn man. None had any apparent ties to the anonymous number or to Lucas. Andy has no reason to believe any of them were involved in the murders. Nothing pertaining to Lucas was found during consensual searches of the residences where the shootings occurred. Unless Andy can locate the phone, it would be next to impossible to determine who made those calls or whether that person had anything to do with the murders. Maybe it was a red herring.

Ironically, the last call Lucas received was from Andy at 9:00 last Thursday night. It was moments before Lucas murdered Ronald. Having missed Lucas at the motel, Andy decided to call and try to convince him to turn himself in. He also hoped to preempt whatever Lucas might be planning to do that night. Lucas didn't answer and Andy didn't leave a message.

Andy has other cases that require his attention, as his captain keeps reminding him. Unless new evidence emerges, his conclusion is that Lucas acted alone. Lisa will not be charged for killing Lucas. She was clearly defending herself and Ronald at their home. Andy signs the report.

Andy's next task is to share his findings with Lisa, Cody and the families of Brian and Russ. He calls Cody first and gets his voicemail. Andy leaves a message briefly summarizing his findings. He ends by telling Cody to call if he has any questions. Truth be told, he'd just as soon not talk to Cody again. Cody was less helpful than he could have been, and Andy will not mind doing him a disservice.

Andy calls Brian's parents in Kansas. He tells them the guy who killed Brian is dead and the case should soon be closed. He also tells them that a note found in Brian's home indicated that he had loaned Cody King $100,000, and it's unknown whether any of it was repaid. He adds that Brian's murder was unrelated to the loan and if the family wants to pursue repayment it would be a civil matter. Brian's parents thank Andy for his efforts.

Next, Andy calls the parents of Russ Nichols in Cleveland. He tells them the man who killed their son is dead. He tells them he's sorry for their loss. They express their gratitude.

Finally, Andy calls Lisa Turner. They have spoken several times since Ronald's death, so his conclusion is no surprise to her. She has no questions, and the conversation is quickly terminated.

Lisa puts down her phone and resumes sipping her caramel macchiato. She is sitting in the New Tampa Starbucks. After Ronald was killed, the rest of that night seemed like a blur. The police arrived within minutes, closely followed by Fire Rescue. They covered both bodies after resuscitation attempts failed. Forensic technicians started processing the scene. Lisa called Ronald's sister Susan and asked her to notify family members. She called Lee and asked if he could come to the house and help her deal with the police. Lee arrived just before Detective Barlow got there. The three of them went into the house where Andy interviewed her. He asked her if she knew who the other man was. She said he was wearing a mask. She put her hand over her mouth when he told her it was Lucas Ward.

Lisa had been sitting in the courtroom when Ronald testified at the trial of Richard Crump. She had never seen Ronald testify, so she decided to be there for his last appearance in court. During a recess, she was returning to the courtroom when she heard Lucas make his homicidal threat. She became alarmed and reported it to a bailiff. He told her not to worry, explaining that empty threats were not unusual in the criminal court process. She had not shared this with Ronald because she did not want to cause him needless concern.

Lisa told Andy about the threat. She described the bailiff whom she informed. She told Andy that when she heard the shots, she grabbed the Ruger and ran to the garage. Andy asked why Ronald did not have the gun and how she got there so fast. She replied that she was more alert to the potential danger than Ronald. She wondered aloud whether police protection could have made a difference. Andy asked about their marriage, finances, life insurance, etc. Lisa answered truthfully, with the exception of denying knowledge of infidelity. After forty-five minutes, Lee asked if they could wrap it up. After all, Lisa had to start planning for her husband's funeral. Andy nodded agreement. "I'm sorry for your loss."

Members of both families helped Lisa make funeral arrangements and settle financial affairs. Her brother and sister-in-law stayed at her house, so she did not have to be alone. The memorial service was held on Tuesday. Lee and Susan delivered eulogies. Their voices broke as they talked about their idyllic childhoods and enduring relationships. Ronald's mother was inconsolable, as was the nephew who had been his godson. Some people expressed astonishment that Lisa seemed to be holding up so well. Her family returned to Georgia on Wednesday. She had taken the entire week off from work but planned to return on Monday.

Lisa rises from her seat to dispose of some trash. The refuse includes the last remaining piece of the prepaid cell phone used to communicate with Lucas Ward. She had dismantled the phone and taken it to the safe deposit box at the bank the day after Ronald was killed. She kept it there until after her house was searched. She then retrieved it and disposed of the pieces in different public garbage cans over the past few days. She sits and resumes drinking her coffee, relieved the ordeal is behind her.

While at work on the Thursday before Memorial Day, Lisa's receptionist told her she had a call from Shana Parker in San Diego. Lisa was simultaneously puzzled and amused. She told the receptionist to put the call through.

"This is Dr. Turner. Is this my husband's TV girlfriend?"

"What? Did he already tell you?"

"Tell me what? I was the one who called you his girlfriend when you worked at Channel 13."

"Has he told you what happened?"

"Told me what?!" Lisa was getting annoyed.

"Let me start over. There's no easy way to say this. I slept with your husband on Sunday night when he was in San Diego."

Lisa was stunned. She stayed silent for a moment while recovering from this bombshell.

"Hello?"

"I'm still here. I just don't know what to say to that. He said he saw you at the convention center, but then you left."

"Well, I'm calling to tell you the truth about what happened. First, I want to apologize. My head was in a bad place. My husband left me and the divorce became final last week. Your husband saw me at the convention center. We started talking and I invited him to dinner."

"Did you go to dinner with him and his friends?"

"No. It was just the two of us."

"I see."

"I had one glass of wine too many. We went back to his room and it just happened."

"Did you know he was married?"

"Yes. I saw the ring and he told me about you. I should have just gone home, but I didn't."

"How did you wind up going to his room? Did he invite you?"

"No. I left my backpack there so I wouldn't have to take it to the restaurant."

"Did you really need to do that? Or was that just a pretext to go back to the room?"

Shana sighed. "I don't know. Like I said, I was in a bad place."

"Who initiated the sex?"

"Definitely me. He hesitated at first, but then he was more than willing. To be fair, I don't think too many men would have resisted. I was pretty aggressive."

"Spare me the gory details."

"Okay. I think we both regretted it right away. I know I did, if it helps."

"It doesn't. Why are you telling me this?"

"My husband cheated on me. I thought you deserved to know. I would have wanted somebody to tell me. Again, I'm really sorry. I'm not a woman who steals husbands."

"No. You just borrow them."

"Fair enough."

"How did you find me, anyway?"

"I'm a reporter. It wasn't hard to track down Dr. Turner at the Bay Pines VA."

"Well, you can lose this number. I'm glad you told me, but I don't ever want to hear from you again."

For the rest of the day, Lisa tried to keep her mind on her duties. The more she thought about the betrayal, the madder she got. While driving home she thought of nothing else. She felt her heart beating oddly, arrhythmic. She had always taken the position that adultery was an unpardonable act. Had it happened early in the marriage, she would have immediately sent Ronald packing. The situation was more complicated after twenty-six years. Their finances were intertwined in a way that would make it difficult to unravel and divide the assets. What if they both wanted the house? Members of both families would be devastated by news of a divorce. To her surprise, Lisa found herself thinking, *Things would be a lot simpler if he would just die.*

Then Lisa remembered Lucas Ward. Did he really want to kill Ronald? If so, she might not even have to pay him to do it. She decided to find out. In the meantime, she would not let on that she knew about Ronald's faithlessness. Would he confess and apologize? Maybe he could still redeem himself. Though it would be difficult, if not impossible, to ever forgive him.

When Ronald closed his office, he brought home files of his recent cases and locked them in a cabinet. Lisa knew where he kept the key. As soon as he left for the grocery store that Saturday, she opened the cabinet and found the file. She came across a witness list where she found Lucas Ward's name and telephone number.

Lisa knew better than to contact this stranger using her cell phone or home phone. She put on a baseball cap and sunglasses and drove to a Wal-Mart, a place she had often said she'd never be caught dead. She paid $57 in cash for an unlocked phone with unlimited minutes for thirty days. She decided to place the call from a spot several miles from her home. She drove about fifteen miles north to a public park in Pasco County. She obsessed for almost twenty minutes before dialing the number. Lucas answered on the third ring.

"Hello."

"Is this Lucas?"

"Yeah."

"Lucas, my name is Lisa. I'm married to Dr. Ronald Turner."

"Who's that?"

"He's the psychiatrist who testified for the defense at the trial of the man who murdered your daughter."

"Okay. So what do you want with me?"

"We have something in common."

"What's that?"

"We both want to kill Ronald."

"What makes you think I want to kill him?"

"I heard what you said outside the courtroom. You said you'd kill him if he helped that animal get away with murder. Well, that animal got away with it. Your daughter's dead and the animal won't spend one day in prison for it. He might even go free in a few years."

"You sound to me like an undercover officer. I think you're trying to set me up. I'm gonna hang up unless you tell me who you really are. How'd you get my number, anyway?"

"I found it in Ronald's case file at home. You can ask all the questions you want, but I am who I say I am."

"Why do you want to kill him?"

"Because I'm married to him. It's personal. But believe me, I have my reasons. The important thing is that you'd like to kill him, and I can help you do it."

"Let's say I do it, and I'm not saying I am. What's in it for me?"

"You mean besides justice for your daughter?"

"That's right."

"What do you want?"

"Money."

"How much?"

"How much can you afford? You're probably rich. It'll cost me at least a couple hundred dollars to get a gun."

"I'll cut right to the chase. I can get you $10,000. Anything more than that and I'd have to leave a paper trail. That's it. Take it or leave it."

Lucas thinks for a moment. "I'll take it. How do we do this?"

They had difficulty reaching agreement. Lisa did not want to meet Lucas in person and refused to consider an advance payment. He didn't trust her to pay after the fact. He suggested that they stage the murder as a robbery. She agreed. She told him what she knew about Ronald's daily routine in the early days of his retirement. Most of his time was spent at home, but she was adamant that Lucas was not to enter their residence. She suggested he ambush Ronald when he left for the gym or the grocery store. Lucas balked when she acknowledged that on none of those occasions was Ronald likely to be carrying more than $50. She offered to hide the money in the trunk of Ronald's car, but Lucas wasn't confident he could quickly find it.

When Lisa mentioned the Thursday night poker game, Lucas was intrigued. He pressed her for details. She was reluctant to divulge her home address and tried to convince him to choose another setting. She understated the amount of money likely to be present. She exaggerated the size and fitness of the other players. She raised the possibility that one or more of them could be armed. Lucas still believed the poker game provided the best opportunity to achieve their mutual goals. He suggested that he invade the home during the game, rob the players and shoot Ronald once he'd secured the cash. Lisa refused and repeated her insistence that he was not to enter their home. Lucas acquiesced, reasoning that it might be unwise to attempt to act alone against eight adult males. Lisa proposed an alternative. Ronald's routine was to clean up the poker room after the game. At half past midnight he would roll the trash bin from the garage to the curb for pick-up the next morning. Lisa said she would place the money in a small trash bag and drop it into the bin. Lucas would lie in wait for the game to end. When Ronald left the garage Lucas would shoot him, take the money and flee. They ended the conversation and agreed Lisa would call again two days later to finalize the arrangements.

Lisa drove to Pasco County to call Lucas on Monday, which was the Memorial Day holiday. Lucas said he wanted to add a twist.

"You heard what I said at court."

"That's right. That's why I called you."

"Well, I said it to Melanie, Sabrina's mother. So she knows what I said. She'd turn me in in a heartbeat. And somebody else could've heard me. If your husband gets killed out of the blue, sooner or later they'll get around to suspecting me. And I won't have an alibi. And if there's physical evidence, I'm cooked."

"So what are you saying? Are you saying you won't do it?" Lisa was half hoping he would back out.

"No, but I got an idea. Why don't I rob one of the other players first? That'll just look random. And I can get some extra money that don't come out of your pocket. Then, a week or two later I kill your husband

and make it look like another robbery. It'll just look like someone scoped out the poker game."

"I don't know. Two robberies means double the chance to get caught."

"Yeah, but we won't be suspected like we would if it was just your husband."

Lisa thinks for a moment. "If you did another robbery first, you wouldn't kill the guy, would you?"

"Not if he does what I tell him to do. But I ain't going back to prison. If he makes me kill him, I'll kill him."

"I don't know. Let me sleep on it. I'll call you tomorrow after work."

Before going home, Lisa stopped at PetSmart to buy a crate, a litter box, cat food and cat litter. Then, she drove to an animal shelter to finalize the adoption of Sneakers. She and Ronald had always agreed that any major life decision required mutual consent. The arrangement had resulted in both of them giving up things they wanted, but Lisa believed she had sacrificed more. No longer. Lisa wanted a cat, and Ronald would have to deal with it for as long as they remained together. It would be her first act of retribution.

The more Lisa thought about the idea of Lucas robbing another player, the better she liked it. If he were to commit the act at another location, it would be helpful in deflecting suspicion away from her. She was uneasy about the prospect of someone other than Ronald being killed. Over the years she had grown fond of David, Scott, Matt, Dick and Robert. All were married with children. She counted their wives as friends and had often socialized with them. She could not bear the thought of feeling responsible for harm befalling any of them. On the other hand, she had no such affection for the game's newer players.

Lisa called Lucas while driving home from work on Tuesday. She told him she agreed that he should rob one of the other players first. She wanted the robbery to occur far away from Hunter's Green. She provided the names, addresses and vehicle descriptions of Brian Ridge, Cody King and Russ Nichols. All of them lived in South Tampa. All were childless and only Cody was married. She suggested that Lucas target Brian. He was usually the first to leave the game and, since he usually won, he would probably be carrying a lot of cash. She did not tell Lucas that she harbored personal animosity toward Brian. His womanizing was offensive to her. Shortly after he began playing in the game, she introduced him to an attractive young internist from the hospital. A few months later the woman told Lisa she liked Brian and she thought the relationship had promise. Then, she brought him to a hospital party and Brian left with a nurse named Jamie. She never heard from him again. If Lucas was going to kill one of the other players, Lisa wanted it to be Brian.

Lucas agreed that Brian seemed to be the ideal first victim. Lisa confirmed that Brian was expected to attend that week's game, which would take place two days later. She verified that he drove a Mercedes convertible and that he usually left the game at 11:15. She told Lucas to wait near Brian's home and ambush him there. Lucas did not like the idea of waiting near the scene for an unspecified period of time. He preferred to wait outside the Hunter's Green neighborhood for Brian to leave the game. He would then follow Brian and rob him at his home. Lisa reluctantly agreed. She suggested that he take Brian's cash but not his credit cards, since a card transaction might be caught on video. He said he would take the cards and dump them somewhere. They agreed that on the second Thursday she'd give Lucas a gate code belonging to neighbors who were moving that week. The code would not expire until the end of June. Lucas would enter the neighborhood and wait inside the gate for Ronald to take out the trash. He would kill Ronald and collect the $10,000.

That Thursday, Lisa made sure to arrive home from work on time. She sometimes greeted the players as they entered, but that night she wanted sufficient time to eat and take a shower so she could watch TV in the bedroom without being disturbed. She did not want to see or talk to any of the players, especially Brian. She told Ronald she was tired and would be going to bed early. She usually fell asleep by 10, but that night she planned to stay up later. She was too anxious to sleep even had she tried. When she heard the front door open and close at 11:17, she hoped it was Brian leaving. She spent the rest of the night tossing and turning.

Lisa was driving home from work the next afternoon when Ronald called her from the police station. He told her Brian had been killed at his home, apparently during a robbery. Ronald did not know any other details. After expressing appropriate shock and sorrow, Lisa asked what would happen with the poker game. Ronald said he wouldn't know until he talked to the guys.

A chill ran through Lisa. It was one thing to talk about somebody being killed, but she was unprepared for the reality to hit her that hard. For a moment she thought she would be unable to see the plan through. She considered offering Lucas $10,000 to call it off. Then, she conjured a mental image of Ronald clumsily realizing his mid-life fantasy in a missionary position with Shana Parker. Lisa regained her resolve. The next day she drove to Pasco County and called Lucas. They agreed to proceed as planned.

The second Thursday was supposed to be Ronald's last. Lisa left work early. While driving she called Lucas to confirm. He warned her that if the money was not in the trash bin, he would come inside the house to get it. She assured him it would be there. She got to the bank before 5 and gathered the $10,000 they kept in a safe deposit box. Ronald rarely visited the box. And he wouldn't notice the missing money if he were dead. She arrived home at the usual time, ate dinner with Ronald, took a shower and got into bed. During dinner she resisted the urge to say anything resembling parting words. Once the game started she took a trash bag containing the money, slipped into the garage and dropped the bag into the bin. At 11:23 she heard the front door open and close. Shortly after midnight she heard several players leave. Trembling, she anticipated the sound of a gunshot. It never came. At 12:36 she heard Ronald arm the security system. He crawled into bed about twenty minutes later. She experienced a combination of puzzlement, anger and relief. She got very little sleep. In the morning she forced herself to rise at the usual time and drive to work. Before she left, she opened the trash bin and saw the bag with the money. She retrieved the bag and tossed it into the trunk of her vehicle.

Ronald called Lisa later that morning to tell her Russ Nichols had been murdered. She was mortified without having to feign it. He said the detective advised them to put the poker game on hiatus. After the call ended, she sat in disbelief. *Why had Lucas deviated from the plan? Was he going rogue?* She decided she needed to put a stop to this. She called Detective Barlow that afternoon to ask about police protection. She called Lucas while driving home.

"Hello."

"What the hell happened last night? You've got some explaining to do!"

"I know."

"We had a plan! Why didn't you stick to it?"

"When I got to the gate, I couldn't get it to open. I tried three or four times. Then I saw the Jaguar leaving. I knew it was one of the other guys you told me about. I figured I'd follow him and get an extra payday. I tried not to kill him, but he left me no choice. And then the asshole didn't have no money! He must have gone broke at the game. So that pissed me off, all that for $4! Don't worry. I'll take care of your husband next time."

Lisa was livid. She screamed into the phone. "There's not going to be a next time! Your bonehead move took care of that! You've killed two people, but not the one you were supposed to kill. Now the police see the connection to the poker game, so they're not going to play for a while, if ever! We might even get police protection."

"So what do we do?"

"There's nothing to do! You just need to lie low. I'll call you if I change my mind, but right now I feel like we're done."

"Yeah, well that don't work for me. I'm due $10,000, and I'll get it one way or another." He hung up before she could reply.

Lisa spent the next several days pondering what to do next. Ronald confirmed there would be no more poker games for a while. That was fine with her. She did not want to afford Lucas the opportunity to kill anyone else. She didn't even want him to kill Ronald anymore. Her desire for retribution was offset by her horror at the growing body count. Her main objective was to put Lucas on a leash until she could decide how to deal with him. Maybe just give him $10,000 if he promised to leave town. But what if he came back for more? She felt like a mad scientist who had created a monster she couldn't control.

Lisa called Lucas while driving home from work the following Wednesday.

"Hello."

"Hi. I just want to make sure we're on the same page."

"Okay."

"There won't be any poker games for a while, so you can take some time off from robbing and killing people."

"Hey! Don't get high and mighty with me. This was all your idea in the first place."

"It was my idea to kill one cheating husband, not two innocent people!" Lisa raised her voice before toning it down. "But that's neither here nor there. There's no game so there's nothing to do but sit tight for now."

"Well, that don't work with my schedule. I'm ready to get this done. I've got to leave town next week."

"Where are you going?"

"I've found summer work in Alaska. So I want to get my $10,000 and get out of here. And when the Alaska job's done, I'll find someplace else to live. I've got no reason to come back here."

Lisa was pleased to hear that Lucas was leaving the state. A chance to cut ties.

"Let's just call it off. You've got the money you took from Brian."

"Yeah, but I want that $10,000 you promised. And we both still want him dead."

"I'd rather just call it off. We've got no time. And without poker we've got no plan."

"Let's use the same plan. He'll still take out the garbage tomorrow night, right?"

"Right."

"I've already got a gate code. All you gotta do is put the money in the container and let me know when loverboy leaves the house to take it out."

Lisa paused. That was actually pretty straightforward. Still, she was not ready to commit. "Not this week. I need to think about it. I'll call you next week."

Lisa did her best to put the matter out of her mind. On Thursday she slept through the night for the first time in weeks. The next morning Ronald called to tell her about the incident involving Cody. Her reaction was authentic. She was incredulous that there had been another robbery attempt. She was relieved that Cody and Cindy were okay, especially now that she knew Cindy was pregnant. Then, Ronald told her Cody had been able to provide a description of the suspect. Another witness saw the vehicle. There was blood that would be submitted for DNA analysis. Detective Barlow told Cody there was a good chance the suspect would be identified soon. Lisa struggled to pretend that was good news.

After the call ended, Lisa sat in her office deep in thought. *I can't put off dealing with Lucas any longer.* It was only a matter of time before he got arrested, either for these crimes or something else. He would not hesitate to betray her if he thought he could help himself. He was a threat to ruin her life regardless of whether he killed Ronald. She was going to have to allow him to get close enough to Ronald to try to kill him. When that happened, she needed to be there to kill Lucas. By the end of her session at the firing range she had become pretty accurate with the Ruger. She hoped her performance could be duplicated in a real-world situation. She saw no other choice.

On Saturday, Lisa drove to Pasco County and called Lucas.

"Hello. I thought I'd be hearing from you."

"Yeah, my husband told me what happened. I'm sorry you struck out again. I hear you got bit by the dog. How's your arm?"

"You care about that? I figured you'd be mad."

"No. I think this actually helped. Now that you've done it three times, they'll never figure it was somebody after Ronald all along. But it's time to get it done. Cody described you and other people saw your car, so you need to leave town soon."

"Did they find any blood?"

Lisa hesitated. She was afraid he'd bolt now if he thought they had his DNA. Then she'd have to worry about him coming back some day.

"No, nothing they could use. You should be in the clear once you do this and get out of town."

"Okay. So what's the plan?"

Lisa said they should revive the idea to ambush Ronald when he took the trash bin to the curb on Thursday night. She said when there was no poker game, his routine was to perform the task at exactly 9 p.m. She instructed Lucas to arrive by 8:45 and park inside the gate. She would call him when she heard Ronald turn off the security alarm to take out the garbage.

"I'll ring once and hang up. Park close enough to get there in a minute or two. And shoot him enough times to make sure he's dead. Empty your clip if you have to. The last thing I need is to be saddled with a living corpse that'll drain all my time and money."

"You got my money ready?"

"It'll be in the garbage bin. After you kill him, just take it and go. And don't get any ideas about coming in the house. As soon as I hear a shot, I'm calling 9-1-1. We keep all the doors and windows locked. The police will get there before you can get in. And if either of us gets arrested, we're both looking at the death penalty or life in prison."

"We won't have no problem if the money's there."

"It'll be there. Is 10,000 enough for you to leave town for good? I don't want you coming back in a year saying you want more. I'd rather give it to you now."

"Well, more would be better."

"Here's the deal. I can get my hands on 15,000. That's it. And then I'll never give you another red cent. You'd have to kill me first. And I put a letter in the safe deposit box that fingers you if anything happens to me. Are we good?"

"That's good."

As far as Lisa was concerned, the amount might as well have been $1 million. She had already returned the $10,000 to the safe deposit box. She had no intention of making a large withdrawal, which would draw attention and leave a paper trail. Since Ronald was not playing poker, it would be difficult for her to slip the money into the bin without him knowing. If she succeeded in killing Lucas she didn't want to have to scramble to recover the money and hide it before the police arrived, especially if Ronald wasn't dead. She would have to gamble that she could end the nightmare by killing Lucas. Whether Ronald was going to die had become a secondary consideration.

When the fourth Thursday arrived, Lisa took pains not to deviate from her usual schedule. She worked a full day and left at the usual time. While driving home she called Lucas to verify that the plan was still a go. She and Ronald ate dinner together. She tried to steer the conversation to benign topics and away from the incidents. She skipped her usual glass of wine, so as to keep her wits about her. Ronald was excited and eager to tell her about his success at the Hard Rock. Still, he seemed lost facing another Thursday night without poker. After dinner, he sat in his recliner and searched the DVR for something to watch. If he was concerned for his safety, he didn't show it. At 8:00, she told him she was tired and was going to bed.

Lisa went to the bedroom and made sure the Ruger was loaded. She took a shower, put on pajamas and got into bed. She waited for the sound of the security system being disarmed. It came at 8:59. Her heart started racing. She tried to call Lucas, but the call didn't go through. She tried again with the same result. Unbeknownst to her, Detective Barlow was calling him at that exact moment. She hid the phone in a drawer, put on a robe, grabbed the Ruger and hurried to the garage. She didn't know whether Lucas was coming or not.

When Lisa entered the garage, it was dimly lit by the bulb connected to the opener mechanism. She turned off the light and crouched behind her Audi. She watched Ronald walk to the curb while rolling the bin in front of him. Seconds later, he turned and started running toward the garage. Lisa moved around the vehicle to the front of the garage, trying to stay out of sight. She counted five shots as bullet fragments and sparks peppered the driveway and the garage. After the fifth shot was fired, she heard the sickening sound of bullet hitting flesh and bone. Ronald screamed in agony and fell on his face, blood streaming from his left hip. Lisa knew Lucas had one shot left, provided he hadn't reloaded. She heard the sound of his footsteps as he walked up the driveway. She heard him fire another shot. Then she heard a click. She stepped out of the garage and fired.

Lisa knows Shana Parker is a loose end. She could make trouble if she hears about Ronald's death and tells what she knows. Lisa is prepared to deal with that if it happens. Until then, she will live the life of her choosing. She decides to stay at Starbucks and take advantage of the free WiFi. She finishes her coffee drink. She has saved a morsel of her muffin to take home to Sneakers. With Ronald gone, she's thankful to have a cat for company. She's also thankful that she and Ronald had not yet cancelled their $2 million life insurance policies. After retiring, Ronald joked that he was worth more dead than alive. Turns out he was right. Susan said she would help file the claim.

Lisa continues browsing sites listing beachfront properties in Pinellas County.

Acknowledgments

FIRST AND FOREMOST, I extend gratitude to my lovely wife. I was attempting to develop a non-fiction book about the murder defendants I evaluated during almost thirty years of practice in forensic psychiatry. Some cases I wanted to include were off limits because there were still appeals to be heard. She suggested I try my hand at fiction. I decided to forego subject matter that would require research. Instead, I chose a familiar topic. A retired forensic psychiatrist hosts a weekly poker game. I added the element of players getting murdered and that was my story. I then spent four years struggling to complete it. My lovely wife remained supportive even after I rejected her suggestion to stimulate sales by revealing the killer to be a werewolf.

Jonathan Greenstein and Rich McIntyre provided valuable feedback on early drafts. I incorporated some of their suggestions to turn a rudimentary story into a more complex one.

The actual Brian Ridge acted as an unofficial editor for several of the later drafts. He helped me see that the first two chapters were heavy on exposition and light on plot advancement. He assisted me in adding story elements and dialogue. He injected fresh ideas when I was stuck. He also enlisted the services of his learned mother, Mary Ridge. I appreciate her insight as well.

Tim Taylor, my youngest brother, provided helpful suggestions on the interviews conducted by Detective Barlow and Lee Turner. My sister Brenda donated sage legal advice and tireless marketing efforts.

Gary Nager was kind enough to write a nice review in the *New Tampa Neighborhood News.*

Phil Scheidt, a family friend, was generous in imparting the benefit of his experience in writing and publishing a first book. His most helpful suggestion was that I consult John Reinhardt for book design. John guided me through the process and made the book look better than I could have imagined. He also recommended Kathleen Strattan as an editor. Her contributions proved to be invaluable.

Most of the events depicted in the book are fictitious. None of the murders are based on actual events. Lucas Ward and Richard Crump have backgrounds resembling those of many criminal defendants I evaluated, but neither is based on any specific individual. The minor characters are fictitious as well.

Regarding the major characters, Ronald Turner is a slightly taller, slightly more successful version of me. Our biographies are similar. I like to think I am a little less rigid and possess a little more humanity. Lisa is loosely based on my lovely wife, although Lisa has a little less sweetness and a lot more venom. Her biography is mostly fictitious. The descriptions of my parents and siblings are superficially accurate, but the book does not fully capture the strength of our family bond. Lee Turner is an approximate composite of my brothers Kevin and Tim. Tim is an accomplished poker player who once cashed in the championship event at the World Series of Poker. He sometimes plays in our weekly game. In the book I did not include Lee in the poker game because I didn't want to inject an element of sibling rivalry.

Regarding the poker game and its players, I have hosted a weekly game for over thirty years. Some of the jokes and conversations in the book are based on memorable quotes from our game. The poker action is fairly representative. Some of the depicted hands are based on hands that have occurred in our game or in local poker rooms. In the book, the stakes and the implied incomes of the players have been magnified for dramatic effect. I thought readers would be more interested in a game where people won or lost $2000 rather than $37. The players in the book are based on regular players in our game. There are enough similarities that anyone who knows them will quickly recognize them. There are also differences and inside jokes designed to elicit a smile. For instance, the substance-addicted Cody King is based on a player who has never used drugs or consumed alcohol. Also, nobody in our game plays as poorly as Cody or Russ.

I should emphasize that the actual Brian Ridge is a much nicer person than the character based on him. Brian is a good poker player, though not as good as his character. On the other hand, when several members of our group entered an event at the World Series of Poker, Brian was the last of us to be eliminated.

Two of the characters are included to pay homage to deceased players. Detective Andy Barlow is loosely based on Randy Marlowe, who moved to Texas to be near family before succumbing to illness in 2016. Randy never ran out of jokes or smiles. Max Dertke would have regarded Jason Bowen as his evil twin. A gentle soul and a card-carrying ACLU member, Max would have been amused at the thought of being portrayed as a career military officer, a Republican Party fundraiser and a Second Amendment advocate. Max did his best to contribute grace and culture to our unrefined group. We lost Max in 2019.

D. R. Taylor